Maltese

Joe Fulda

Betsy Siino

BARRON'S

Contents

Meet the Maltese: An Introduction

Take a look into the bright, black button eyes of the Maltese. Though you seem to find the sparkle of a decidedly contemporary sprite, that sparkle actually emanates from an ancient soul with an innate understanding of the human species. What follows is an exploration of the world of Maltese dogs and their place within the human family, all in an effort to ensure that they receive the care, adoration, and understanding they deserve. Whether you are a veteran of Maltese companionship or a newcomer to the fold, here's hoping you enjoy the journey.

A PERSONAL REFLECTION

Before we begin this journey, let me first confirm my qualifications to lead such a trek, as I have lived a large chunk of my life with these tiny dogs. My first Maltese came to my family when I was about ten years old. After living most of their lives with larger dogs, my parents unexpectedly found themselves captivated by a tiny Maltese belonging to some friends—their first contact with a dog of this breed. Unable as they were to get the little guy out of their minds, they surprised us by welcoming a new Maltese puppy into our family shortly thereafter. An adorable, scruffy little thing with a snowy white coat and lemony ears, this tiny creature would become one of the most legendary dogs of our family history.

As anyone who has shared the privilege of living with a Maltese can testify, there is nothing quite like the spell one of these vivacious spirits can cast on a household. This breed indeed has the power to change lives. Our "Tiger," as we named that first Maltese of ours, would indeed come to have that effect on us.

When we speak now of Tiger, which we so often do, we remember his quiet, gentle nature that somehow belied a heart worthy of his namesake within. We remember a courageous, intelligent dog who survived a physical confrontation with a coyote (with scars to prove it), who regularly chased renegade tarantulas around the deck in the backyard, who played shortstop in makeshift baseball games with my brothers, who loved the wind in his face as he rode in a speedboat on a mountain lake, and who rotated where he slept to ensure everyone got equal time with a Maltese foot warmer at night.

So quiet and complicit was our boy, always seeming to understand whatever scheme we had planned for him, that he remained still and silent whenever we would sneak him in to no-pets-allowed venues, from the Disneyland Hotel to various western ski condos to large indoor shopping malls. The only time he escaped his role as contraband was at Los Angeles International Airport, when he wriggled free of my mom's coat—where he was hiding—to chase after my little brother who himself had given chase to Paul McCartney, who was being chauffeured to his gate in one of those golf-cart-style airport vehicles. My brother knew nothing of the Fab 4, but he had to get a closer look at that little indoor car. Tiger just knew that where my brother went, fun would follow, while Sir Paul—chased as he was at that moment by a little train of boy, white fluffball, and a mom—was probably presuming his fan base, formerly throngs of squealing teenagers, was now far more eclectic—and canine—than it used to be.

Anyone who has shared the privilege of living with a Maltese can't help but smile at such tales, for all who have shared in this honor have their own legendary tales to tell. As part of this family, we share an innate understanding

of a toy dog that actually embodies the term "lionheart." We understand the effect of the indomitable spirit of the Maltese and what it means to have a Maltese in the family. The Maltese boasts a large and devoted following, and a large and devoted family, all of us knowing that we would probably not be the people, let alone the dog people, we are today were it not for the influence of these tiny white creatures in our lives.

AN IRRESISTIBLE TOY

Live with a Maltese for any length of time, and you join an illustrious club of Maltese fanciers that spans back thousands of years.

You are also bound to discover just how a dog that weighs in at all of 7 pounds (3.2 kg) has commanded such a fierce following for so many decades—and so many centuries—and continues to do so today.

The Maltese is among the more glamorous of the American Kennel Club's (AKC's) classification of dogs known as the toy breeds, and, in keeping with his nature and his history, he is quite at home being referred to as "the aristocrat of dogs." For many centuries, Maltese have been companions to people of culture, wealth, and fastidious tastes, thus accounting for the breed's own reputation for refinement, fidelity, and

Love of Miniatures

Humans, it seems, have always held an affinity for miniatures, whether that be miniature houses, miniature horses, or, yes, miniature dogs. As soon as humans learned to breed domestic animals selectively for individual traits, they set about miniaturizing the large working dogs that were gaining a reputation for friendship with their kind into more suitable household companions. This would ultimately result in the dogs we now know as the very popular toys, dogs who possess physical characteristics and temperaments identical to those of their larger brethren, but in smaller, more convenient packages.

Take a look at the Pug, for instance, and see the influence of Mastiff-type cousins in both the face and fearless demeanor of the smaller version. Or consider the Pomeranian. Were it not for his diminutive size, you could certainly imagine the Pom—with his pricked ears, smiling face, thick double coat, and plumed tail—pulling a sled through the Arctic like his sled-dog cousins from whom he was bred. Nor do you need to guess where the long, spindly legs and speed of the Italian Greyhound came from, or why the Cavalier King Charles Spaniel insists on chasing songbirds on her daily walks. Pit a Toy Poodle against her larger cousins in the confirmation show ring, and the only difference you're likely to notice is size.

We all come from somewhere and someone. The same applies to our toy breeds, most of which leave no secret as to their illustrious origins. You might say that within the family of toys, we can see represented the entire history of dogs and their relationship with those earlier humans who decided most fortuitously to make these animals our best friends.

cleanliness. This timeless breed continues to enjoy such reverence today in our more democratic times as well, gracing the homes of folks within all levels of society.

In addition to the loyalty he commands, today's Maltese also closely resembles his illustrious ancestors, presenting much the same image today, described in the official AKC breed standard for the breed as a dog covered "from head to foot with a mantle of long, silky, white hair." But, beyond this glamorous visage, this ancient breed continues to embody a fine collection of characteristics passed down through the ages from all the Maltese that came before.

Those who are just now becoming acquainted with the Maltese are in for a rare and delightful experience in dog keeping. Note the use of the word dog *keeping* rather than dog *owning*, as no one truly *owns* a Maltese. Individuals fortunate enough to spend time with one of these dogs usually agree that at some point in the relationship, the revelation of just who runs the show becomes clear—and that "one" usually has four tiny white feet.

THE MALTESE'S TOY STORY

Though we have a fairly solid idea of *how*, much conjecture exists over just *where* and *when* the Maltese came to be. We know this little gem of a dog boasts an ancient lineage spanning back thousands of years: six to eight thousand, say some, in regions of the world as diverse, say others, as Asia and Egypt. We will, however, stick with the breed's more modern history, begun about 2,000 years ago, when artists, writers, and philosophers began to immortalize dogs of Maltese charm and the description on the island of Malta (from which the dog takes his name); the Sicilian town of Melita, which some claim to be the breed's true home; and even Greece and Rome, where the Maltese was depicted on works of art dating back to approximately 500 B.C.

Though we may never know the full story of this breed, the earliest accounts from such luminaries as Aristotle (the fourth century B.C.), Pliny the Elder (50 A.D.), and Saint Clement of Alexandria (the second century A.D.) speak of dogs with obvious Maltese charms, accounting, it would seem, for the Maltese's value as a hot commodity along early European and Mediterranean trade routes. Maltese have endured throughout history as companions installed in the laps and tucked into the sleeves of fine ladies from ancient Rome to Elizabethan England (having come to England during the reign of Henry VIII). This dog has also held the position of favored muse for such renowned artists as Sir Joshua

What's in a Name?

Given a history that spans back thousands of years, the Maltese has been known by a vast collection of names, depending on who was claiming ownership of the breed during any given age. He was at one time the "Melitae Dog" to those who claimed the breed hailed from the Sicilian city of Melita, while those in the Malta camp preferred "Ye Ancient Dogge of Malta." Both "The Comforter" and "Maltese Lion Dog" would seem accurate names for Maltese both ancient and contemporary, while "Maltese Terrier" would seem less than accurate, since the Maltese is more likely a descendent not of Terriers but of Spaniel and Spitz lines.

Reynolds and Sir Edward Landseer, the latter for some reason predicting, while working on a portrait of a Maltese in 1840, that the breed was ultimately destined for extinction.

As we know, of course, Sir Edward's prophecy of doom would go unfulfilled. Shortly after the famed painter made his prediction, the Maltese began what would become an illustrious and enduring show career with his first appearance in the British show ring. This would extend to America later in the nineteenth century, where the breed would be recognized by the American Kennel Club in 1888 and take the country by storm, both as pet and Best-in-Show contender. The Maltese has thrived stateside ever

since with show people and pet homes alike, also becoming—and not surprisingly—a favored fashion accessory and pampered pet to Hollywood A-listers, the "A-est" of these being the late Elizabeth Taylor.

MALTESE CHARACTER

The exact origin of this tiny "white-mantled" pup may be somewhat obscure, but that means little to anyone who shares life with the Maltese today. Through the ages, in Maltese homes everywhere, memories are made and linger of a glamorous imp; a bold but good-natured family member; a frolicsome, people-loving companion, who, by any standard, is the quintessential "good thing" in a (very) small package.

Maltese tend to be joyful little critters who like to think that whatever they are doing, even if that is obeying commands in an obedience class, is their idea, or at least the result of a team decision. In other words, instead of forcing him into submission, be patient with your Maltese as you work gently with him toward your common goal, and respect his uncanny understanding of our species, forged, as we know, over thousands of years.

Many today know the Maltese as a loving family member. Dog show folks know him as a formidable competitor. Intruders have discovered the Maltese to be a courageous and alert alarm and ankle biter. Men, even the beefiest of body builders, often find themselves unashamedly drawn to this breed's outgoing, fun-loving heart and take one as their own—a twist of fate they may have never expected from a pampered toy. Indeed, it seems our privilege as a species to enjoy the company, the attention, or even just the appearance of the Maltese dog. Whatever the circumstance, encounter a Maltese and, odds are, the incident will be memorable.

An Ancient and Opinionated Soul

The Maltese holds some rather set opinions about life. What seems to suit his family in the way of comfort usually suits the Maltese as well. This can be a wonderful breed for elderly and solitary people, for apartment dwellers, and for quiet households, but the Maltese can also thrive in a home where growing, active kids are being raised (and taught to treat the family dog kindly and gently).

This dog is not typically enthusiastic about changes in routine, sloppiness, or exile from family gatherings. Because of his small size, the Maltese is probably not the ideal canine companion for toddlers, either, though if children in the family understand the word "gentle" and are well schooled in dog play protocol, the Maltese can be a lovely play-mate with proper adult supervision.

The Maltese can also enjoy rousing games with other dogs, including much larger canine playmates (again, supervision is required). Besides the size difference, the Maltese is all dog. He may not be able to leap tall buildings in a single bound, but he can do just about anything his larger four-footed, fur-bearing canine cousins can do, and he often exhibits profound leadership abilities while doing it.

One such Maltese comes to mind that used to frequent a park near this author's home. This tiny 5-pound (2.3 kg) slip of a thing would sit regally ringside while my 80-pound (36.3 kg) Samoyed played with the 80-pound (36.3 kg) American Pit Bull Terrier who shared the tiny Maltese's household. Once her majesty decided the jousting had gone on long enough, she would walk delicately forward and just stand beside the gladiators, who would instantly stop, as though called to salute. And thus we would witness the true definition of the title "Queen Bee."

What Every Maltese Owner Needs to Know

With the grand mission of placing Maltese dogs in forever homes, Southern Comfort Maltese Rescue offers the following pieces of advice that those considering bringing a Maltese into their lives should consider.

- Maltese can bark a lot and thus are prone to separation anxiety.
- The Maltese must be made a full-fledged member of his family.
- Maltese are indoor dogs. They must be carefully supervised outdoors, as they can fall prey to other dogs, coyotes, and even birds of prey.
- A Maltese should be walked with a harness to protect his small neck and to prevent the incidence of a collapsed trachea, a condition common to this breed.
- Because of their size, Maltese are not necessarily ideal for families with small children, unless the dog will be carefully protected 24/7 from rough handling or accidental injury.
- Maltese can have knee problems, common especially in dogs who jump down from furniture and stairs all day.
- Maltese require diligent attention to their coats, ears, teeth, and eyes to keep them clean and healthy.

Maltese mature slowly; enthusiasts often claim that these dogs remain puppies longer than most dogs, especially toy dogs. Those looking for a couch potato canine, then, may need to look elsewhere. Despite his diminutive size, the Maltese enjoys all the activities typically associated with people/canine relationships: taking walks, learning tricks, and accompanying mom or dad on errands in the car. He is a curious, intelligent, adventurous, very demanding little bundle of energy and friendship; quiet and sensitive if that fits the mood of his human companions at a given time; or dynamic and playful should that be more appropriate.

Though quite adaptable if family is near, these dogs do not appreciate being wet, and they cannot tolerate extremes in temperature. The Maltese is indeed very sensitive and responsive to his environment, and thus requires great understanding from his family regarding his preferred comfort zone. Assume, for example, that your pet will not enjoy being left alone; gentle and consistent patterns of behavior on your part, indicating to the dog that you will return soon, go a long way toward establishing a relaxed dog, an absence of separation anxiety, and an everlasting bond. Male and female Maltese are equally affectionate and have clean and regular toilet habits when properly trained and socialized, and both have the potential of being lovely, well-mannered companions.

BREED-SPECIFIC CHALLENGES

Every breed is endowed with its own special characteristics and challenges that make its care unique within the world of dogs. The Maltese is no exception.

The Maltese will be a non-tax-exempt dependent on his owners for twelve to fifteen years, and, all in all, should experience few health problems with proper care. Though Maltese health is addressed in greater detail later in this book, discuss with your dog's veterinarian early on the incidence of heart murmurs, liver shunt disease (when the blood flow bypasses the liver), and potential respiratory troubles in Maltese dogs.

You must also stay vigilant in checking your Maltese's ears. Those long, heavily feathered ears can be a friendly environment to yeast, parasites, or bacterial infections, but if you keep your pet's ears clean and dry—

and watch for signs of ear scratching, head shaking, and foul odors—you can stay ahead of budding problems. Pay attention to "rear end" cleanliness as well. Inspect your Maltese regularly to make sure fecal matter doesn't get trapped in the fine hair back there. Such a condition can block easy elimination and ultimately lead to some serious problems down the line, so keeping the back end clean makes life more pleasant for everyone involved.

Another frustrating aspect of Maltese keeping is managing the tear stains that so often appear on the adorable white faces of these cuties. This occurs from runny tearing that stains the hair beneath the inside corners of the dog's eyes, most often the result of a sinus infection, allergies (which can also cause the dog to lick incessantly at his feet), dental problems, or eyelash abnormalities. Whether runny eyes are caused by age or the physical condition of the dog, they should be treated, both to enhance the comfort and ultimate health of the dog and to rid unsightly red-to-brown staining on that sweet face.

And, finally, many Maltese enjoy barking. On the bright side of this, they can be fine watchdogs, alerting the family and everyone else within hearing distance that someone has just rung the doorbell. Some also bark for the sheer joy of barking, all in keeping—it would seem—with the bold and vivacious nature of a dog who does not care to be ignored but who should be trained to curb that behavior as well. Just remember, this is a dog who loves and needs to be with his people. Satisfy this goal and help your pet understand when enough is enough, and barking will be far less of a problem.

Not for Everyone

Despite their charms, the fact remains that the Maltese, and toy dogs in general, are not the ideal companions for everyone. Would-be dog owners are often naturally drawn to the convenient size, beauty, and cuteness factor of the toys, but, when considering any breed, they must also evaluate their lifestyles and families. Taken together, these factors may prove to be incompatible with, or even dangerous for, such a small dog.

Even those who, after careful consideration, decide a toy dog is for them may not be an ideal match for a Maltese. For example, a dog weighing in at 4 to 7 pounds (1.8–3.2 kg), in keeping with the Maltese breed standard, may actually be too small for a family with very young children, a herd of careless teens, or a house full of other rambunctious dogs

and animals. The same holds true for a family seeking a toy who will be reliably obedient and quiet. The headstrong nature and penchant for barking evident in so many Maltese may be more than a family can or wants to handle.

And, of course, there is that signature silky white Maltese coat, a coat that requires more than occasional attention. Though that coat, and the lively black button eyes peering out from the mantle of white, may draw one initially to this breed, that mantle of white comes with a greater degree of responsibility in terms of time, effort, and money than the casual admirer may expect. While the aesthetic characteristics of this breed are appealing, the beauty of the Maltese, and the demands of the little character that comes with it, may not be enough to hold the bond between person and pet together.

Wise Choices

So you've decided you just may want to be owned and manipulated by a Maltese. Next step: Start gathering information about the breed, speak to breeders, study the Maltese breed standard, and seek out those who live with Maltese; all of this will prepare you to make a wise and informed decision about the dog you invite into your home to turn your life upside down.

SMART DECISIONS

The most important ingredient in selecting and caring for a dog of any breed is common sense. Despite the tug an adorable ball of fluff may exert on your heart, use that brain of yours to consider all the consequences before you take the plunge.

First, consider the details. Whether you will be acquiring a full-grown adult or a Maltese puppy, continue to do your homework, learning all you can about the Maltese, even from Maltese owners you find walking their dogs on the street who just may offer you some valuable insight about living day-to-day with one of these dogs. While you're at it, review the American Kennel Club (AKC) standard for the Maltese breed, and even attend a dog show or two to chat with breeders about your interest and to see the breed standard come to life. Purebred AKC dogs are bred to a blueprint, or standard, that describes the ideal specimen in terms of both anatomy and characteristics. Once you have seen the standard come to life in a variety of Maltese dogs, you may be better prepared to choose a Maltese that will fit your lifestyle and family.

Exploring the details also means considering any limitations that might be imposed on your new relationship by your lifestyle—and vice versa. If you live in an apartment, for example, providing your puppy with daily exercise and waste elimination will be an adjustment you'll have to make. Of course, you'll also have to confirm you can have a pet—even a tiny dog—not to mention a tiny dog who can get a little yappy.

Consider a prospective pet's age as well. Puppies are irresistible, yes, but when acquiring one, evaluate the investment of time and money you'll need to make to shepherd that adorable ball of fluff toward becoming a beautiful, well-adjusted adult Maltese. You may decide that an adult dog who may already be house-trained and obedience-trained would be a better choice, and, indeed, there are Maltese of all ages in need of good homes.

WHERE TO FIND YOUR MALTESE

Though an ethical, reputable breeder (not to be confused with the "backyard breeder," who hopes to make a few bucks off the family pet or create a project for the kids) is a fine source for a Maltese, this is not the only source for loving, companionable Maltese dogs. What follows should help clarify just where you might find your new companion— and what sources you should avoid.

The Reputable Breeder

Just what is a reputable breeder anyway? A reputable breeder is a person who has studied all aspects of a breed, who works to enhance the breed's quality, and who helps to educate potential buyers while making the finding of proper and permanent homes for his or her puppies the highest priority. In short, the reputable breeder is someone who has devoted his or her life to the dogs he or she loves; someone who is active in breed, canine, and/or rescue organizations; and someone who embraces the national breed club's Code of Ethics.

About the Maltese Standard

The American Kennel Club breed standard for the Maltese calls for a dog of 4 to 7 pounds (1.8–3.2 kg) who is covered with "a mantle of long, silky, white hair." His tail should be a "long-haired plume carried gracefully over the back," and he should sport "drop ears" that are "heavily feathered" as well as eyes that are "very dark and round, their black rims enhancing the gentle yet alert expression." The Maltese should move with "a jaunty, smooth, flowing gait," his straight, pure-white coat cascading almost to the ground.

The Maltese should be "gentle-mannered and affectionate" yet "eager and sprightly in action, and, despite his size, possessed of the vigor needed for the satisfactory companion." The Maltese should seem "to be without fear." In sum, he is "among the gentlest of all little dogs, yet he is lively and playful as well as vigorous."

The standard, then, offers would-be Maltese buyers and adopters a clear picture of who the Maltese is meant to be. Armed with this knowledge, you will be far better prepared to choose your new little companion with a clear and informed head.

The breeder we are describing here will address honestly with potential puppy buyers any undesirable characteristics of the breed and the challenges those would-be new owners might face, such as that of caring for the beautiful Maltese coat. If you are that would-be owner, he or she will provide you with references and welcome your questions. You might ask, "What made you choose the Maltese?" Or "How long have you been breeding these adorable dogs, and what problems might new owners encounter living with them?" This breeder will be quick to answer your questions and will be pleased the questions are being asked.

The reputable breeder will also invite you for a site visit to meet his or her puppies and dogs and to show off the environment in which they are being raised. This breeder's Maltese will be sold with a contract addressing genetic screening; spaying and neutering; Limited AKC Registration for pet-quality pups (meaning should those pets be bred, their puppies cannot be AKC registered); and a clause stating that if there is a problem, the dog must return to the breeder (a reputable breeder cannot tolerate the idea that one of his or her dogs will end up abandoned and homeless).

Locating a Reputable Breeder

Word of mouth is probably the most valuable tool for finding a reputable breeder (or any canine professional), so start collecting recommendations. First stop: local veterinarians. Given the popularity of the Maltese breed, you may be surprised to find veterinarians who have several Maltese breeders to recommend in your community—though you will still need to do your own "vetting" of those prospects. Plus, many veterinarians own, and even show,

purebred dogs themselves, so the veterinary community is typically plugged in to the local kennel club.

This brings us to the next logical source of information: the local kennel club itself as well as other dog clubs in the area, which, with any luck, boast local Maltese breeders and enthusiasts as members. For obvious reasons, grooming shops are also great sources of information for finding breeders of Maltese in your area.

Once you have collected names of Maltese breeders in your area, arrange to visit them. As we have seen, clean facilities, a willingness to answer questions, and an obvious familiarity with the breed are good signs, as is a breeder's adherence to the

American Maltese Association's Code of Ethics, which, among other tenets, states that Maltese puppies should not be sold before twelve weeks of age. You should also value a breeder's curiosity about you, too—evidence of a commitment to ensuring that his or her puppies go to the right homes with the right families.

As always, let common sense be your guide. A breeder who suggests you meet in a store parking lot should raise a red flag. Someone has something to hide, so don't even think about working with such an individual. Once you make initial contact, you should be more than welcome to see the living conditions of the Maltese you are considering. By the same token, beware of breeders (and

shelter staff members or rescue volunteers) who don't grill you about your home and family situation (apartment or house? children? other pets?), your dog experience, or how you intend to care for your new pet. An uninterested breeder is probably just trying to make a buck and does not qualify for that all-important "reputable" title.

Shelters and Breed Rescue

The Maltese is adorable and captivating and has charmed the human race for thousands of years. But, sadly, no breed is immune from the trauma of pet overpopulation and homelessness, and the Maltese is no excep-

tion. Enter, then, the possibility of finding the Maltese companion of your dreams at the animal shelter or through a Maltese breed rescue group.

For any number of reasons (the kids were too young and careless, the owner died, the novelty wore off, etc.), perfectly wonderful purebred dogs—Maltese among them—are abandoned or surrendered to shelters and breed rescue groups every year. And every day the dedicated people who run these organizations find themselves fostering little treasures just waiting to be wonderful companions to families that will love them and keep them forever.

Evaluating the Online Maltese World

Type the word "Maltese" into a search engine, and you will be flooded with websites for Maltese breeders, Maltese rescue organizations, and pet websites that provide lists of kennels with Maltese for sale. Indeed, view the Web as a valuable resource, but in doing so, remember that anyone can say anything on the Internet, whether it is true or not, so prepare to navigate with head over heart. Keep the following tips in mind:

- Don't be snowed by a glitzy web design. A skilled Web designer has no connection to healthy, well-adjusted, properly socialized Maltese dogs.
- Steer clear of "breeders" who offer a wide variety of breeds. This is a sure sign of a commercial puppy mill or similarly large-scale puppy "factory" operating solely for profit.
- If you find a kennel that looks promising, make contact, ask questions, check references, and set up an appointment for a visit. Despite what you find touted online, the kennel visit is the only way to evaluate its size and cleanliness, as well as the character, skill, and devotion of its proprietors. The Internet can be great for opening doors, but bring your discovery to a personal level as quickly as possible.
- Ask if the breeder is licensed by the U.S. Department of Agriculture (USDA). A "yes" answer is a red flag, in that the breeder may be running a puppy mill, licensed as required by the USDA to sell puppies to brokers or pet shops.
- Just as you must grill the breeders you meet with questions, make sure they quiz you back. A reputable breeder, both online and in person, will want to know as much about his or her puppy buyers as those buyers want to know about their prospective pup's breeder. Get your questions answered and get those clear guarantees before, during, and after the sale. Reputable folks, online or in person, won't hesitate to comply.

Choosing a rescued Maltese (usually an adult) is no different from choosing one from a breeder. Ask questions, find out everything you can about the prospective pet's background (former family situation, reason for surrender, health issues, behavioral quirks and challenges, etc.), and remain on guard with your common sense in tow. The Internet can be a great tool in the search for rescued Maltese in need of new homes, bringing prospective adopters into contact with rescue groups and rescue dogs all over the country, but resist the impulse to make your ultimate choice out of pity.

Top-flight rescuers get to personally know their second-chance dogs to ensure that this

time they land where they are meant to be. But remember, "rescued" does not mean "free." To fund their good works, shelters and rescue groups must charge adoption fees, which can be several hundred dollars. This supports not only the everyday care of the dogs in their charge but also any veterinary care or rehabilitation their dogs might have required in preparation for adoption, as well as for spaying and neutering, as all shelter and rescue dogs should be altered dogs once they go off to their new homes. Beware of rescuers who don't insist upon this and who fail to interrogate you about your intentions, your dog ownership history, your expectations, and your lifestyle. Unfortunately, while well intended, some rescue groups are so overwhelmed with dogs that they may not take the time required to ensure their charges are properly placed.

WHERE NOT TO FIND YOUR MALTESE: PET STORES AND PUPPY MILLS

That Maltese charm that has captivated humans for millennia can be a double-edged sword. Though that charm has made Maltese as beloved today as yesterday, it has also made Maltese hot commodities, appealing to those disreputable types who see these dogs as a means for making a quick buck.

Those who love dogs have had the unfortunate experience of seeing little balls of fluff rolling around in the window of a mall pet store, surrounded by crowds of adoring fans. The rise of large pet supply stores that sell supplies but no puppies has rendered such scenes less common than they once were, but pet-store puppies, and the massive "puppy-mill" breeding operations that supply them, still exist, banking on the impulses of people willing to buy that cute doggy in the window—with no experience, no forethought, and no preparation necessary.

While the pet store puppy may be adorable, odds are he was bred without proper housing, care, nutrition, and genetic screening of mom and dad within a cold, austere, possibly filthy environment. Odds are mom has been bred during every heat cycle to optimize production, and odds are her pups were taken from her long before the optimum eight- to twelve-weeks of age (twelve for Maltese) to optimize their cuteness factor for marketing purposes.

So yes, you may find that pet store puppy adorable. Or you may even consider purchasing him out of pity. But in doing so, you are only feeding the beast that relies on people purchasing puppies without preparation or forethought, that has no concern for the care the puppy might or might not receive in his new home, and that is unconcerned about any health

Health Checklist

Note the following when evaluating potential Maltese pets:

- Look for general good-health conditions: alert, bright eyes; overall clean look and smell; and clean nose, ears, and feet.
- Skin and coat: Rub patches of fur against the direction they lie and look for red skin, bald patches, or flaking skin. The coat should be uniform and fluffy.
- Observe the puppy walking and running, and look for lameness or other abnormalities.
- Inquire about initial vaccinations and deworming. By fourteen to sixteen weeks of age, the puppy should have had one or two rounds of puppy shots.
- Ask to see the puppy's dam and, if possible, his sire, and any siblings that might be available, too.
- Ask about health screenings and registration papers. Whether working with a breeder, shelter, or rescue group, make sure you can take the dog to a veterinarian for a health check within the first few days to confirm the dog is as healthy as he seems—with the right to void the transaction if he is not.

problems that may lay in wait. By resisting that impulse to purchase the pet store puppy (or the puppy directly from a puppy mill), the buyer helps to reduce the demand that keeps puppy mills churning out puppies—and thus reduces the suffering of the dogs at the heart of such operations as well.

THE BIG DECISION

If you think educating yourself about the Maltese and the people who breed, rescue, and care for this breed is a monumental effort, brace yourself. The most difficult task of all is at hand: the actual selection of your new pet.

Selecting a healthy pup should be your primary concern (see Maltese Memo: "Health Checklist"). Consider, too, how age affects health. According to the American Maltese Association's Code of Ethics, Maltese puppies are best placed at twelve weeks of age, and conventional dog wisdom says don't even think about separating a pup from his canine family any earlier than eight weeks.

For proper physical and emotional development, puppies require sibling interaction, a good dose of TLC from mom, complete weaning from maternal dependence, and their first round or two of puppy immunizations, all of which take place in this twelve-week time period for this slowly developing breed. Temperament evaluations are more accurate with a ten- to twelve-week-old Maltese, plus puppies of this age are better able emotionally to adapt to a new human family at this age than are younger pups.

Meeting the pups' mom and dad is also valuable, offering you a glimpse of what the little balls of fluff cavorting around your feet

and tugging at your shoelaces (and your heart) will look like, and perhaps even act like, in a year or more. Meeting mom can be especially illuminating. Mom's influence on her progeny is critical during her puppies' first weeks of life, as she teaches them what it means to be a dog. Sweet, gentle, attentive moms tend to raise sweet, gentle, well-adjusted puppies.

Look for the healthy puppy, yes, but also for the pup you like and who likes you back. Here, the Maltese breeder (and Maltese rescuer, too) can be a big help. Discuss your lifestyle, your family, and what you envision your long-term relationship with your new pet to be. Good breeders know their puppies. Good rescuers know their second-chance fosters. They know that each has a distinct personality, and they can help guide you toward finding the perfect match.

SHOW QUALITY OR PET?

A common misconception exists among the general public that because a dog is registered with the American Kennel Club or other canine registering body, that dog is a show-quality canine. This is not true. Registration papers simply document that the parents (both sire and dam) were issued registration numbers as a certain breed, that their parents and grandparents were registered, and so on. The basic principle of registration makes it possible to track the heritage of a purebred dog and to assure new owners that their acquisition is indeed a purebred.

The description of a dog as "show quality," on the other hand, is intended to describe a purebred dog with attributes that, when judged by an acknowledged authority, con-

form to what is accepted as the ideal standard of the breed. A registration certificate cannot guarantee a dog's quality; it only shows that the dog's parents were also registered purebreds. In fact, there is no guarantee that because a puppy's parents were champion show dogs, the puppy, too, will be destined for a successful show career. Indeed, more often than not, out of a litter of five puppies born to dog show title holders (sire and/or dam), only one or two of the puppies might turn out to be show quality. Sometimes even the most carefully matched breeding pair does not produce even one show puppy.

Do not, however, write off those adorable pet-quality puppies or view them as inferior in any way! They may not meet the nuanced ideals of a breed standard apparent only to a veteran show ring judge, but they are beautiful nonetheless and, like their show-quality siblings, the beneficiaries of the same high-quality breeding program. For show- and pet-quality alike, when a dog—any dog—is cherished by a loving and responsible family, the role of protector, companion, lap warmer, and champion of the backyard is just as important as satin ribbons and shiny trophies. Show quality is nice, but it must always take second place to a dog's role as beloved companion and family member.

INTELLIGENT EVALUATIONS

Just a warning: As difficult as it might be, steel your heart when it comes time to meet a group of Maltese puppies, one of which just might be your new best friend. Indeed, "Heaven on Earth" is probably the most accurate way to describe the experience of

sitting on the floor with a group of tiny white black-eyed puffballs rolling around, yipping for your attention, bouncing up as best they can to lick your ear, scrambling all over each other to be the first one to your lap. How can you possibly choose?

First, try to see those little puffballs as the individuals they are. Hold them in your arms, and see how they respond to your touch (and expect that one or two might be shy, which need not be a deal breaker). Roll them over on their backs; those who struggle are of a more dominant nature, while those who are perfectly content in that position are more submissive; both can make lovely companions when properly matched. Evaluate which are more or less mouthy (puppy hand nibbling is normal), and handle their feet to determine which accept this willingly

or would rather pull their paws away. And, of course, listen to what their breeder has to say.

Use similar "tests" for evaluating adult Maltese candidates, although adults will require a bit more caution. They may have had negative experiences that don't detract from their ability to be fine companions but may affect their responses to traditional temperament evaluations from strangers. Listen to those who have been caring for the dog (shelter staff, foster parents, breeder, etc.), as they should be able to guide you through the process and determine if a particular dog is a match. Indeed, the ultimate goal of all devoted Maltese caretakers—whether show breeder, foster mom, or shelter volunteer—is to shepherd their dogs into homes where they will be nurtured and cherished for the rest of their lives—a goal that you will now share as well.

A Maltese in the Family

Bring a Maltese into your home, and into your heart, and life as you know it will never be the same. Whether you welcome a puppy into your family or adopt an older dog (a dog from a shelter or breed rescue group, or a retired show dog from a breeder), the first few days, or even weeks, will be a time of transition and perhaps even frustration. But soon, with sound preparation, consistency, and patience, you'll find yourself reveling in the new rhythms of the household and probably won't even remember what life was like without a Maltese in the house.

BRINGING YOUR MALTESE HOME

Once the wheels are set in motion, and you know that a Maltese—puppy or adult—will soon be joining you, preparing for your new pet's arrival can help ease the natural stress and, yes, even trauma, that can result from the dog's transition from one environment to another. There will be adjustments for everyone, of course, but Maltese are adaptable creatures when their needs (and their comforts) are met by sensitive, well-prepared owners. If your new family member has nutritious food, comfortable shelter and bedding, clean water, and properly measured attention waiting for him, it will take only a short time for him to settle into your routine.

So what preparations should you make before your new Maltese companion comes home? First, figure out where your new pet will be sleeping. Set aside a quiet corner of the house that can be his private, comfortably appointed sanctuary. This can be a cushy dog bed, an exercise pen, or a dog crate (preferably not your bed—at least until the dog has matured, both as a dog and as a family member who understands his place in the pack hierarchy).

Next, gather up the family and take a trip to your local pet-supply store to purchase your dog's supplies (hard to beat this as a fun family outing!). To begin, you will need:

- Food and water dishes (whatever food the dog has been eating).
- An appropriately sized buckle collar and, if possible, a current identification tag (which your pet should wear at all times; even a tiny lap dog that spends most of his time indoors needs proper identification).
- A properly sized harness for walking on leash (safer for the tiny dog's neck and throat).
- Safe chew toys.
- Puppy treats.
- A dog crate and/or exercise pen.
- A lightweight leash or lead (nylon or leather, no chain).

It will be your job to convince your new friend that his new environment among this new family of his is going to be even more comfortable and loving than the one he is leaving behind. The dog's former caretaker can provide information on your new pet's eating habits, the food he is currently eating, and every other element of his life to date. The more information you have about where your pet has been, the easier it will be to bond with him and overcome any problems you might encounter while establishing that bond.

COUNTERACTING STRESS

When you first bring your new Maltese companion into your home, your goal is to maximize his comfort and contentment while maintaining your own domestic tranquility. What follows is an overview of what you'll want to avoid:

- **Overstimulation.** Excessive handling or an introduction to too many new sights, sounds, activities, and adoring fans can create stress and insecurity.
- **Overfeeding or underfeeding.** Poor feeding habits can cause diarrhea and malnutrition. Keep snacks healthy

and moderately offered, and feed on a schedule, so the dog always knows when and where to expect his next meal.

- **Lack of attention.** Find the happy medium between overdoing and avoidance—too little attention can bring on anxiety and related behavior problems.
- **Neglecting training.** Start your house-training regimen immediately to reduce accidents. Do the same with basic obedience to ensure your Maltese becomes a polite, confident—and safe—canine citizen. A dog who knows what is expected of him, who understands boundaries, and who is offered the opportunity to please his family, is a much happier dog.

- **Shared sleeping.** Permit a tiny dog to snuggle in with you under the covers at bedtime, and you could roll over on the little guy and cause serious injury. An overly bossy pup may also get the message from such an arrangement that he is your equal and can behave badly if he so chooses. Provide your dog with his own secure corner of the world, even if this is simply his crate or bed installed in a corner of your bedroom floor.
- **Toys with bells, squeakers, or other small parts.** Puppies and small adult dogs can swallow or choke on those small toy attachments, with painful, sometimes surgical, consequences.

HOUSE RULES

Just as critical as gathering supplies and equipment for your new pet before his arrival is the need to establish the house rules, which, to some, aren't often considered all that important in a house that is home to a dog so small. It's a mistake to believe this, as household, family, and dog will all be more comfortable when everyone is behaving properly.

As we have noted, decide first where the dog will be sleeping, arrange his bed, and be ready for a few sleepless nights in the beginning. Set ground rules as well for what and when the dog will eat, and establish "treat" protocols. Make sure everyone understands that it is not cute or funny to sneak a piece of birthday cake or a slab of leftover steak to your tiny friend, as this can lead to life-threatening obesity and obnoxious behavior. Commit as a family to healthy treats only, which are to be offered in moderation as rewards for training, or as part of the daily routine, such as just before bed or before you leave the house for work.

Rules should apply to furniture protocols as well. It is the rare Maltese who is not allowed free access to the household furniture, but try to prevent your dog from jumping from couches, chairs, and beds, perhaps by teaching him to wait for you to transport him into your lap and down again. A fearless acrobat can end up suffering from knee problems common in this breed. He might also injure his back, neck, and ligaments by leaping haphazardly around furniture and tearing down the stairs, so teach your Maltese that good things come to those who wait.

PACK COMMUNICATION

Dogs communicate with each other by scent, body language, and eye contact. Through their powerful sense of smell, dogs—both large and small—can determine the gender, temperament, and intentions of every dog they encounter. They also use body language to convey their own attitude, temper, and intent to others, as well as to advertise their particular positions in their family packs.

The way the dog is carrying his ears, a slight movement of the lips away from the teeth, the tensing (or relaxing) of the body, and the position of the tail are all signs a dog uses to send messages that can be interpreted by other dogs. Also expressive is the band of hair that runs down the middle of the dog's back, which will stand upright, or bristle, when a dog is angry or assuming a defensive posture. This "puffing up" is intended to give the impres-

Maltese and Babies

Though the Maltese is not typically named an ideal breed for young children, many do coexist peacefully and safely. This usually requires not only supervision of both parties but also early preparation. With proper preparation, training, and introductions, Maltese and baby—and ultimately Maltese and child—can become life-long friends. The following can help ease the transition:

- Before the baby's arrival, take an obedience refresher course. This strengthens the bond between dog and owner and also helps to fortify your dog's sense of security and understanding of acceptable behavior.
- Put a stop to such behaviors as biting or nibbling on hands or ankles. Provide plenty of chew toys instead.
- Introduce your Maltese to friends' babies and well-behaved children to accustom your pet to the movements and voices of young humans. Better yet, plan ahead: When raising a puppy, socialize the young pup to children by introducing your pet to as many carefully chosen dog-friendly kids as you can during his first year of life and beyond, making sure that your dog has only positive experiences with youngsters.
- Allow your pet to investigate a blanket or similar item that carries the baby's scent before you bring the baby home.
- With careful supervision, allow your Maltese to sniff the new baby when he or she first enters the household.
- Make sure your dog continues to get plenty of attention and exercise as you all adjust to the new baby in your home, and reward him profusely for sitting or lying quietly beside you as you feed and tend to the baby.
- Include your pet in daily walks when you take the baby out for a bit of fresh air.
- For the safety of all, never leave the dog and the baby (or any child) alone and unsupervised, and teach your child as he or she grows that only gentle treatment of the family pet is acceptable.

sion of greater size and formidability, though, frankly, no matter how puffed up a Maltese becomes, it is doubtful the word "formidable" would ever come to mind.

Eye contact is another important means of communication for dogs. A direct stare is a challenge in dog language, whereas averted eyes indicate a desire to avoid confrontation. Staring down an aggressive dog, even a tiny one, is not usually a wise move. It is, however, quite rewarding to meet the eyes of a dog who thinks you are the greatest gift to the world—and, particularly, the greatest gift to that dog. The softening and almost smiling glint in the

Now, many of us have had the unfortunate experience of entering a household where the dominant pack member, and thus the pack leader, is the family dog—even a dog who tips the scale at 7 pounds (3.2 kg) and is nothing but a ball of fluff. It's not a pretty sight. Though we have spoken playfully about being "owned by a Maltese," you still need to be the pack alpha—the boss. From the time he comes into your home, teach your dog, whether puppy or adult, his place within the pack with gentleness, love, and clear signals. If a dog knows that his position is recognized and accepted by the other family members, who in turn treat the dog with respect and consistency, you can all live happily ever after.

THE CRATE: A PLACE OF HIS OWN

One area of controversy often found within the world of dog owners is that of the dog crate. Critics of crating typically point to the over-use of crates, where a dog is left "in the box" for long periods of time or is relegated there as punishment or for the owner's own convenience. Such criticisms are certainly justified. Yet, on the other hand, citing the ancient canine habit of living within the cozy confines of dens and caves, proponents of proper crating view it as a valid and effective way of managing and training canine pets, many of whom grow to view their crates as havens of privacy and security and their own quiet corner of the world.

Many a Maltese has come to view the crate in just this way, with the crate, door open or closed, providing a safe sanctuary from all the noise and commotion of the house-

eyes of a devoted canine companion is a measure of love that you would be hard-pressed to duplicate.

Despite his small size, the Maltese is just as fluent as dogs ten times his size in canine language and just as attuned to a pack mentality inherited from the wolves that started it all. With canine pecking order ever in mind, each member of the pack learns and accepts his or her position in the family group, from the dominant alpha on down, creating an arrangement that provides stability and a sense of security to all pack members.

hold and a quiet sleeping place at nap time. Confinement in general is also a wise choice for the management of any dog of any size when the animal is left home alone. Indeed, most dogs—and homes—are safer when the resident dogs are confined somewhere safe in their owners' absence, an arrangement that prevents such mishaps as housetraining accidents and chewed slippers, furniture, and electrical cords.

A crate can also serve as a safe and convenient home away from home when your Maltese joins you for a trip by train, plane, or automobile, and manufacturers have come up with some adorable crate designs for adorable traveling companions. As those who fly know, tiny dogs are often permitted to fly with their owners in the cabin if the dogs are properly crated and behaved. You may then use the crate as a safe and familiar sleeping place for your dog when you arrive at your destination. Hotels, motels, and even the homes of out-of-town family and friends are more receptive to dog owners if they know the dog can be confined quietly to a crate.

Crating also aids in housetraining, as dogs do not tend to relieve themselves where they sleep. Most healthy adult Maltese can sleep crated and "hold it" through the night, or for six to eight hours in the day while their owners are away. Working people might think of expanding the confinement concept to a larger, well-secured exercise pen configuration during the day to allow the dog more room to move and play and stretch his tiny legs. Small dogs can often do well relieving themselves on so-called "potty pads," which you can place in a corner of the exercise pen (or house) while you are away for several hours at a time. The properly appointed ex-pen is a humane confinement option, and one with which Maltese can be quite content.

HOUSETRAINING YOUR MALTESE

One of the most important—and potentially frustrating—stages of your Maltese's training is the dreaded task of housetraining. You need not dread this task if you commit to it properly and take it seriously. Unfortunately, far too many owners of toy dogs often make

excuses for the fact that their companions are not "perfectly" housetrained. Tiny dogs leave tiny calling cards, they figure, so no big deal, right? Wrong. Regardless of size, a properly house-trained dog is a joy, both within the family and beyond, so take the time, commit to the work, and reap the long-term benefits.

Some toy breeds are notoriously difficult to house-train, and Maltese seems to fall into a middle ground here—and often by no fault of their own. As we have discussed, Maltese are slow to mature, and if they join their new families at the recommended twelve weeks of age, they may be better students of house-training because their bladders have matured, as have their bladder-control abilities.

The other issue can be a lack of owner commitment. Yes, it's a pain to have to take the dog out incessantly during those first days of training, but a 110-percent commitment to this "pain" will reap grand benefits before you know it. Though he may be headstrong and opinionated, the Maltese is a fastidious little creature, who, with proper communication and consistency, can be a delightfully competent and cooperative student of housetraining. Establish an unwavering routine that fits your schedule, commit to close observation of your little student, and follow a few simple rules, and having a perfect housetrained Maltese can be achieved.

The Housetraining Regimen

When housetraining, as with all training, keep things positive, reward the dog on the spot for his proper responses, and resist the urge to scold your pup for an accident two hours, or even two minutes, after an indiscretion (and avoid physical punishment or the "rub-his-nose-in-it" technique completely).

Follow these simple steps religiously, and you should find in no time that you are living with a Maltese who not only practices impeccable bathroom habits but also understands just what those he loves expect of him:

1. Take the dog outside to a single familiar, preferably grassy, spot at regular intervals. Don't *put* the dog out. *Take* the dog out on a leash.

2. Suggested times for bathroom breaks are: first thing in the morning, as soon as the dog/puppy wakes up; immediately after each meal, nap, and play session (and remember, young puppies may eat three times a day); and just before going to bed. Yes, you'll be going in and out all day long, but consider this a valuable investment in the future.

3. Observe your dog's body language. Dogs send "potty-alert" signals when they feel the need to go. They start sniffing intensely at certain areas of the floor, and they may appear anxious. The student who is really starting to understand will stand by the door with an uneasy look in his eyes, so make sure you reward him by receiving, and responding to, that message!

4. Encourage the dog with a short command, such as "*Go potty.*" (Choose the command and stick with it.) When the dog relieves himself, shower him with praise. Let him know he has pleased you beyond measure, and he'll look forward to doing it again. If, on the other hand, you take him out, issue the command several times, and he simply will not do his business, don't stay out there forever. Go back in, place the pup in his crate (not as punishment, but to prevent an accident), and a few minutes later, take him out again to repeat the process. Your goal is not to lose your temper or punish the dog, but to teach him a life-long skill.

5. If you do catch your dog squatting on the floor (and every dog has accidents at some time during, and after, the process), shock him to attention with a loud "*Stop!*" (no physical punishment); hoist him into the air; get him outside to your designated spot ASAP; and once he finishes, praise, praise, praise. If you see the accident but not the act, don't even bother scolding the pup. You must catch him during the act, or he simply will not understand.

Housetraining can be time-consuming, and, as you can see, it's wise to bring your new pet home at the start of a weekend or vacation so you'll be home to carry out the task effectively. However, whether you're training a puppy or an adopted older dog in need of a refresher, house-training isn't nearly as difficult as its reputation paints it to be.

With consistency, the older dog should catch on quickly, and as a puppy matures, the day will come when he no longer needs to run in and out all day to relieve himself.

All successful dog training is based on the three Rs: routine, repetition, and reward. Adhere to the housetraining regimen—and every training routine—with these guidelines in mind: Repeat and review every phase of training, and reward your student with praise and, occasionally, a treat. Your personal reward from successful housetraining will come in the strong bond you forge with your dog and, of course, the preservation of your carpets.

Preparing a Training Game Plan

Housetraining is typically a dog's first introduction to the concept of formal training, launching what should be a lifetime of learning. With housetraining as the foundation, do all you can to remain positive and consistent, and see how this carries over into other training areas as well. A dog who learns that proper behavior can earn praise, and who is scolded properly (instantly and without physical punishment) will quickly learn what is expected of his behavior within the family pack. With consistency as his guide, and clear messages received from his people, the newly welcomed Maltese needs to learn that certain actions are always prohibited while others are always encouraged—all of this serving to help your new pet adjust to his new home and bond with his new family.

Maltese are happiest inside the home and close to their family packs, the Maltese mantra being, "Close to you is good, closer is better, and consistently close is best." You, in turn, will probably prefer to spend time with a dog who knows how to behave within the household. Training satisfies you both, offering your dog a mechanism by which he can feel secure and confident, while at the same time helping him to meet what he comes to understand are your expectations of him. We will delve deeper into training in a later chapter, but for now, remember that you are wise indeed to introduce your new Maltese—puppy or adult—to the concept of training as soon as your new family member enters your household.

Feeding a Tiny Dog

Maltese, just like their human counterparts, are what they eat. By instilling proper eating habits in your pup—and proper Maltese feeding practices in yourself—you will better protect your pet's health and overall comfort (and, as we know, Maltese are all about comfort).

BASIC NUTRITION

The pet food industry has grown mightily in the past three decades, with dog food sales in particular maintaining a steady upward trend. But, despite what some of the advertising following that trend may claim, one brand does not fit all.

Proper canine nutrition depends on a number of factors, including the dog's size, activity level, age, and living conditions. Consider, as well, dogs with special nutritional needs, such as high-powered athletes, lactating moms, growing puppies, and dogs struggling with illness. Proper nutrition for all dogs is based on a balance of proteins, carbohydrates, fats, vitamins, and minerals. But that balance differs between a Maltese that spends a great deal of time in his owner's lap with occasional exercise retrieving a ball or chasing a cat, and a 110-pound (50 kg) Alaskan Malamute who pulls a sled for a living.

FEEDING SUCH A SMALL DOG

Canine feeding requirements vary by life stages. These stages are generally indentified as growth (puppy), maintenance (adult), and geriatric (senior). Start your puppy, then, with a quality puppy food, followed at about nine to ten months of age, as your pup's total nutrient requirements begin to decrease, with a gradual transition toward a healthy adult maintenance program.

The way you feed your dog can be as important as what you feed your dog, and this is typically determined by the dog himself. To get a glimpse into how well you are managing your dog's diet and eating habits, observe your pet's stools (fecal matter) on a regular basis. Excessively loose, pale, or foamy stools, or stools the color of your dog's food, indicate poor digestion, while smaller, darker, firmer stools suggest that all is well within your pup's digestive tract. Regular elimination habits are also a sign of healthy nutrition and digestion, as is a glossy, pliant, clean-looking coat and healthy skin.

As for the amount to feed your Maltese, adjust the volume so your pet is neither too chubby nor too thin. Generally, a dog is

overweight if you place both hands around his midsection and cannot feel ribs (unfortunately, a not-all-that-uncommon condition among pampered toys). Your dog is too thin, of course, if you feel skin stretched over ribs that are far too defined to your touch. Seek the happy medium. A preferred weight for a healthy Maltese is 4 to 6 pounds (1.8–2.7 kg), although a larger Maltese (bigger boned) will weigh a bit more. Let your dog's body type be your guide.

Now let's move on to *how* to feed your Maltese. Most adult dogs do well on two daily feedings—morning and evening. If you must feed once a day (and we sincerely hope you can accommodate the twice-a-day option), feed the dog early to allow for optimum digestion and waste elimination, followed by a healthy dog biscuit or two in the evening to take the edge off until breakfast. Make sure your dog's food dishes are clean, and always keep a supply of fresh, clean water available as well.

THE COST-EFFECTIVE/ HEALTH-EFFECTIVE DIET

Improvements in canine nutrition have resulted in our dogs living longer and free of many of the health problems once caused by inferior ingredients that were simply thrown into pet foods because they couldn't be used for anything else. With higher quality nutrition, a dog may need to consume less of his food to maintain a healthy body and mind. High-quality food, then, may indeed cost more, but the health of your Maltese will make up for that cost, and feeding a Maltese is certainly much less expensive than feeding

Essential Nutrients

Every dog requires balanced rations of the following nutrients to maintain a healthy mind and body.

Proteins. Among other functions, high-quality proteins are required to build healthy bone, muscle, and blood.

Carbohydrates. Dogs (and humans) require carbs for energy and proper brain function.

Fats. Another essential energy source, fats must be offered sparingly, preferably only as an ingredient in commercial dog food.

Vitamins and Minerals. These are essential for almost every function of the body, but they must be balanced within the dog's diet. An excess of certain vitamins and minerals can cause severe health problems.

Water. Water is a nutrient, too, so make sure your Maltese has plenty of the wet stuff—fresh and clean—available at all times.

a German Shepherd. Just remember the old adage: You get what you pay for.

Feeding a small dog does not involve some of the health risks inherent in feeding larger dogs, who tend to gobble their food, which can lead to the life-threatening condition known as canine bloat. Nevertheless, it may be wise to moisten your Maltese's dry kibble with a little warm water to help ease its way

down your pet's digestive tract—especially if you have one of those pups who doesn't take the time to chew.

The amount you feed your Maltese is also critical to overall health and condition. You can monitor proper feeding by administering the trusty rib cage test mentioned above and also by weighing your dog periodically. Most, but not all, Maltese are overweight if they exceed 7 pounds (3.2 kg), with 4 to 6 pounds (1.8–2.7 kg) being the preferred weight, depending on body structure and adult size. Determine what is normal for your Maltese, and let that, as well as the recommended portion sizes of the specific food you choose, be your guide.

CONSISTENT FEEDING HABITS

The canine digestive tract typically locks in to particular feeding times and foods, so maintain a consistent feeding schedule, as well as food and water supply, to maintain your pet's digestive efficiency.

Sudden changes in rations can be a shock to your dog's system. To change a dog's diet— for example, when the new puppy or adopted rescue dog joins your family, or when an aging adult is switching to a food formulated for older dogs—add a little of the new product to the older fare. Increase the amount of the new food and reduce the amount of the former food over time until you have made the transition complete. The bottom line: A

bowl of brand X that suddenly and totally replaces the usual brand Y will probably result in brand Z diarrhea.

Dogs don't usually object to a change in flavor as long as the basic diet remains the same, but they don't require constant changes in flavor either. A dog's eating habits are dictated primarily by his sense of smell. That is, it's okay to add a little chicken or beef broth to your little furball's dinner from time to time as a treat, but don't necessarily count on flavor to whet your pet's appetite.

TOO MANY CHOICES

In the last three decades, the pet food industry has experienced a revolution of sorts in consumer education and pet food research.

This has resulted in an explosion of the number of high-quality commercial foods available in grocery stores, in pet-supply stores, and on the Internet—foods that meet standards almost as stringent as those for foods manufactured for humans. Lines of prescription diets are also available from veterinarians to address such canine health concerns as heart disease, urinary tract disorders, and even dental problems.

New to the pet food landscape are fresh and frozen natural foods that actually resemble what we might find on grocery store shelves for humans. These foods, which can be pricey, must often be kept refrigerated both in the store and in your home. Their claims to fame tend to be that they contain a minimal number of ingredients, may be grain-free, and contain actual meat proteins rather than meat meals or by-products. You'll find these foods in the traditional settings (pet-supply stores and even some grocery stores), as well as in specialty stores devoted to high-end pet products.

With so many options, choosing the right high-quality food for your Maltese can be further complicated by the types of foods available; with canned foods and dry foods topping the list. Or, if you are truly courageous and have plenty of spare time on your hands, you can even try making your own.

Canned foods. Canned dog food is appealing to the olfactory senses of a dog, and it is often used by veteran dog owners to flavor dry kibble. About 50 percent of its protein content is from meat, fish, or poultry, and the remaining is derived from eggs, dried milk, and meat by-products, all of which have a high water content. The average can of dog food contains carbohydrates (typically from corn, barley, and/or wheat), as well as a combination of vitamins and minerals. Many owners of small dogs like the convenience of canned food, but it can be costly.

Canned dog food is offered by nearly all major pet food manufacturers for each stage of a dog's development, as well as for various levels of activity and lifestyle. Canned foods have also been developed for adult dogs with kidney, heart, and other health disorders. Although they work well as flavoring agents, canned foods alone are not the best choice for fostering healthy teeth and gums, and they tend to produce soft stools.

Dry dog food. Probably the most popular dog food style, and for good reason, dry dog food usually comes as a complete diet in the

form of kibble, pellets, or flakes. A high-quality dry food is a combination of meat meals, grains, and vegetable products supplemented with vitamins and minerals that, like all high-quality foods of every style, bring the product up to the standards outlined by the Association of American Feed Control Officials (AAFCO). If the food you choose does not state on its package that it meets these standards, choose another dry dog food.

Dry dog foods tend to be the least expensive of the dog food choices. They are packaged in boxes and bags as small as 2 pounds (0.9 kg), which can help keep a small dog's food fresh. Resist the temptation to purchase in bulk for cost efficiency; given a Maltese's small daily ration, spoilage will set in long before you have even made a dent in that giant package.

The Maltese with Allergies

Another topic worthy of attention is the effect of nutrition on Maltese allergies, which are not all that uncommon. If your pet seems far too interested in chewing and licking at his feet, resulting in an unsightly pinkish-brownish tinge on the hair, not to mention obvious discomfort in the dog, your dog probably is suffering from allergies of some kind.

Those itchy paws, as well as eye-staining, may be the result of an allergy to grasses and other vegetation, but a food allergy can also be to blame, as food allergies often cause such symptoms as skin troubles and gastrointestinal conditions akin to irritable bowel syndrome in humans.

Enter another category of foods that, while still balanced and of high quality, contain what we might call odd ingredients—duck or venison, for instance, combined with rice and barley. These foods are designed to introduce unfamiliar elements into the dog's system that do not trigger an allergic response. You may find that such a diet, combined with cleaning your dog's feet in warm water after an outdoor adventure (a quick soak and then drying the feet with a towel), can help keep those allergies at bay.

High-quality dry dog food products are convenient to use and store, are good for digestion (evident in the firm, small stools they produce), and help to keep the teeth and gums healthy. Most professional "dog" people recommend choosing a balanced, high-quality dry food produced with consistent quality, and those who follow this recommendation are rarely disappointed.

Whether you choose canned or dry, commercial or specialty, choose balanced, high-quality foods and feed properly and consistently, and you will do your Maltese a great service. Although every meal of your dog's menu may be the same, each is a measure of

your special attention. Of course, your decision need not be set in stone. If, for example, you choose food that seems to cause poor fecal quality or chronic gastric upset, your dog's system is telling you that a change—a gradual change, remember—is in order. Also observe your dog's energy and activity levels and his overall well-being. If your pup seems happy, robust, internally healthy, and active—with a good appetite, bright black button eyes, and a healthy coat, you have probably made a good choice.

The home-cooked meal. Home-cooked diets are another alternative, and there are indeed folks who choose and commit to this option. "Commit" is definitely the proper word here, for this endeavor cannot be pursued half-heartedly or ignorantly.

Though dogs are omnivores and require a variety of ingredients in their diets, a healthy homemade canine diet requires specialized recipes for the canine palate and system—not a share of whatever the similarly omnivorous human family members are eating each day. The owner who decides on the home-cooked option must therefore become educated about canine nutrition and gain access to the often specialized ingredients required to create a properly balanced canine meal.

To be honest, many (if not most) owners who set out with the grandest of intentions to create homemade food for their dogs ultimately decide to leave the science and art of concocting their pets' diets to the experts. With so many culinary options out there for pets these days, some that almost seem made for the human palate, they need not feel guilty about this change of heart.

DOS AND DON'TS

No discussion of Maltese nutrition would be complete without mention of the dangers of table scraps—yes, "dangers." Unfortunately, far too many dog owners equate loving a dog with satisfying that dog's desire for "people food." This can result in a sad, unhealthy, overweight Maltese who just keeps begging for those tasty morsels.

If you are one of those compelled to share your sumptuous fare with your pup, remember that a dog's digestive system will not function well over the long term on the same foods that we eat. Habitual supplementation of a dog's diet with table scraps not only prevents him from ingesting the proper balance of the nutrients he needs, but it also sends him the message that his eating habits are based on when, where, and what his owners eat, which is not a good message. If you must share an occasional tidbit with your cherub, avoid doing so on a regular basis—and never do so directly from the table. Better yet, when you just can't say no, offer your pup a quality dog biscuit instead.

Contrary to outdated opinion, dogs and bones are not necessarily compatible either. Delicate, splinter-prone poultry, fish, and pork bones are a no-no, but beef bones can also splinter and pose the same choking threats and puncture damage to a dog's throat and insides. And while we're on the subject of potentially dangerous dog treats, please do not feed your luxury-loving Maltese chocolate, either, as theobromine in chocolate can be toxic, especially to such a tiny dog. Experts also caution owners to avoid offering

dogs raw eggs, fried foods, onions, grapes, and desserts of any kind.

In addition to inappropriate treating, many owners are also tempted to tamper with a balanced diet by adding extra fats, vitamins, and minerals, believing that if some is good, more must be better. Oversupplementation of any kind, even with healthy nutrients, can create problems more complex and difficult to diagnose or treat than simple diet deficiencies.

This leads us to another "don't" that is worth repeating again and again: Please don't overfeed your dog. Make sure he receives his proper rations each day to keep him healthy, fit, and spry (and live longer), and make sure he gets plenty of exercise, too, so he can be with you for many years to come.

49

Well Groomed and Bushy-Tailed

Choose a Maltese as a pet, and you're going to be faced with the challenge of caring for that glorious coat. Maltese hair is akin to human hair in terms of maintenance: It requires washing, brushing, combing, and trimming. In addition to the standard nail clipping, dental care, and ear cleaning necessary for every dog, the Maltese's grooming regimen may also include a trim around the dog's feet to keep them neat and around his eyes to keep them clean. If your Maltese is introduced gently and positively to grooming, you'll both be better off.

THAT MANTLE OF WHITE

A Maltese is not a Maltese without that signature white coat, so grooming will play a prominent role in your dog's life. Your goal in this endeavor is to convince your pup that cooperation with the grooming procedures is not only her idea but is also something to be savored.

The coat of the adult Maltese requires daily care and attention if it is to remain mat-free and pristine, and the typical Maltese can, and should, learn not just to tolerate, but to enjoy, frequent brushing and grooming sessions. Helping the dog build positive associations with grooming time is the best way to accomplish this.

Maltese puppies must be taught from a very early age to lie quietly and allow their caretakers to brush and comb their soft, glossy hair; fiddle with their ears; and play with their feet and tails. Be warned, however, that Maltese puppies can be surprisingly strong-bodied and strong-willed, so politely allowing themselves to be groomed may not come naturally to the healthy Maltese. Also, forcing the issue will never work. This pup must learn, through positive experiences, to enjoy the attention that comes from his inevitable grooming sessions, beginning with brushing—the cornerstone of the grooming regimen.

FIRST THING'S FIRST: THE BRUSH

The care of a Maltese show coat—the cascade of white flowing down, flaring out as a fine curtain of silk as the dog, with topknots in place atop her head, traverses the floor— would command an entire book of its own (and it has). Grooming isn't quite so complicated, of course, for Maltese pets engaged in everyday family life, who should still be brushed at least every other day to prevent matting, stimulate skin health, and clean the coat. The longer you wait between brushings, the more likely that lustrous, silky coat will mat and tangle, and the longer and more uncomfortable the brushing session will be.

The Maltese coat can mat fairly easily, and mats can be difficult to eliminate, resulting in painful hair pulling that certainly will not endear you to your opinionated pet. Keeping the coat properly and regularly brushed, then, is the key to preventing mats, though you may not be able to prevent them completely. When you do find mats in your dog's coat (which tend to accumulate behind the ears and elsewhere), it is usually best to cut the mats out, as is commonly done when Maltese are rescued from less-than-worthy homes and

Grooming Tools

To groom a Maltese properly, you will need the following tools:

- Small pin brush with stainless steel teeth
- Small, rubber-backed slicker brush
- 6-inch (15-cm) stainless steel comb with rounded teeth
- Small, portable hair dryer
- Pair of scissors with rounded tips
- 1-pint (0.5 L) plastic water spray bottle
- Shampoo and coat conditioner (formulated for dogs!)
- Small face or pocket comb
- Orthodontic rubber bands for topknots
- Toenail clippers designed for small dogs
- Styptic pencil or specialized powder to stop nails from bleeding if "quicked"
- Canine teeth-cleaning supplies

circumstances. Better yet, stick to the regular brushing schedule and prevent matting altogether.

Begin your dog's life of brushing by first introducing him to the fundamentals. Practice laying him on his back on your lap for a few minutes several times every day until he decides he is comfortable in that position (ply him with treats and praise should he require some gentle convincing). Move on then to rolling him gently over on his side, taking

time to acclimate him to that position as well. In time you can transfer him to a more convenient grooming surface or table, perhaps a thick rug on the floor or your pet's pillow, or you may just decide to keep him in your lap.

Once your pup is completely comfortable lying on his side on the grooming surface (which may also take time, treats, and some sweet talk), introduce the brush. Run it gently through his hair. As you do this, continue talking to your dog to reassure him, and remember that praise is an excellent training aid. If he is amenable, repeat the procedure with the comb. Keep the session short, and try to end on a positive note—with you, not your dog, deciding when the session is done.

If you can't keep up with regular brushing, you may simply choose to keep your Maltese's coat trimmed to a cute puppy length—about 1 inch (2.5 cm) all over—in keeping with the breed's reputation for remaining a perpetual puppy. This easier-care coat style can help to facilitate healthy hair and skin as well, but remember that regular brushing and grooming remains a must.

As a Maltese matures, so does his coat, and required brushing time will increase proportionally with the increase in coat length and density (though brushing remains simpler, of course, for a Maltese with a short puppy cut). For best results, and to ensure the coat is brushed down to the skin, brush in layers. That is, part the hair at the skin and, using the pin brush, brush only the section that is exposed. Part the hair again at another location, and repeat the procedure again and again until you have brushed the entire coat. A spray bottle of water can come in handy during this process, especially in dry environments. A fine mist sprayed on the hair after it is parted (in a coat free of mats, please) can ease the brush's path through the strands. Plus, dampening increases the tensile strength of the hair, which reduces tears and breakage.

To make the signature Maltese topknots, brush the top of your dog's head, then part his hair in the middle of his skull down to the tip of his nose. Now, firmly gather the hair on one side of the head, and make a loop of about ½ inch (1.3 cm), folding the hair backward, away from the dog's eyes. Using a small latex rubber band, secure the fold to make the Maltese topknot. Repeat the procedure on the opposite side of the head, equal to the position on the first side, and you'll have your twin topknots.

Remember to brush and comb the hair on the chest, down the legs, between the legs, and under the tail. Finish by brushing and combing the tail itself. Your Maltese is now ready for a bath if that is where you are headed (but do remove the topknots for the bathing ritual).

BATHING YOUR MALTESE

Maltese can learn to love their baths if they are handled by their bathers with patience and a regard for their safety and security. Secure footing is a must, as are special considerations to protect the eyes and your dog's sensitivities. Though you do not want to get soap of any kind in your pet's eyes, you might try a no-tears shampoo made for dogs in hopes that you won't irritate those big, dark eyes begging you to get the bath over with

quickly. When first introducing your Maltese to bathing, remember, too, that a jet of water spraying out of a faucet or spray nozzle can frighten such a tiny dog, especially a young puppy. Start puppies off by simply introducing them to the water. Sprays can come later.

A bathtub or utility/laundry room sink with a non-skid surface (a simple rubber bath mat will suffice) both work well as tubs. For the procedure itself, there is really no need to fill the tub with water. Instead, once the dog is accustomed to the tub and its surroundings, wet him thoroughly as he stands in the waterless tub. To do this, use a large plastic cup or a shower hose attachment turned to a gentle spray—with water reliably kept at a tepid (lukewarm) temperature—and wet the dog until he is saturated to the skin.

Now apply a ring of shampoo around the dog's neck and ear area, and start lathering. If the dog has fleas, this "chases" them rearward and keeps them away from the dog's face and eyes. Work the shampoo and lather down to the skin, moving toward the rear and applying more shampoo as needed. Pay particular

Seeking Professional Help

It's no secret that the keeping of the Maltese coat can be a challenge, especially if you wish to keep your pet's coat in the long, flowing style of the show ring. Even if you prefer the short puppy cut, the services of a skilled professional groomer can be invaluable, especially to trim the coat without incident to that puppy length.

If you choose to delegate your pup's grooming to a professional, you will want to find someone who is skilled in the care of the unique Maltese coat. Equally important is someone devoted to the kind and gentle handling of your little friend, who could be injured and emotionally scarred by rough treatment. Ask around for references, particularly from people who are clearly devoted to their pets. Speak with a prospective groomer candidate on site ahead of time to evaluate the cleanliness of the shop and the experience of the groomers, as well as their safety practices (for example, drying procedures designed to prevent burned skin and hair).

Just as you did with grooming tasks at home, introduce your Maltese early to the professional grooming experience. Whether you enlist a professional for your Maltese's grooming needs; decide to go it alone; or work in partnership with the groomer—where, for example, you do the routine brushing and bathing while the groomer trims the coat and nails—remember that neatness and cleanliness play major roles in your pet's overall health, comfort, and longevity.

attention to the dog's tummy, private parts, and feet, and work the lather in between the toes and paw pads (hence the benefit of teaching your dog to tolerate handling of his feet). When the dog's body is thoroughly lathered, use a washcloth or soft sponge to wet and wash his face.

The next step is a complete rinsing with that gentle shower hose or plastic cup. To avoid skin problems, never leave soap or soap residue on your dog's skin or coat, so do whatever it takes to remove all those suds. Watch the rinse water carefully, and as long as it continues to run cloudy, rinse again. Once you are certain that your Maltese is ready for drying, turn your head slightly to one side to avoid the ensuing spray of water and prompt your puppy to shake his body as only dogs can do. For some dogs, this occurs almost as an automatic reflex, but others need a little encouragement. Try leaning in close and blowing a few quick puffs of air at his nose. Then back away quickly, or you could wind up wetter than your pet in the ensuing whirlwind of water.

Professional groomers typically recommend that you apply a cream rinse or conditioner to the dog's coat before you begin the drying process. This not only enhances the luxurious appearance and texture of the coat but also helps reduce tangles and matting between baths and brushings. If you plan to follow this recommendation, apply the product generously and work it into the coat. Allow the conditioning agent to set up, and then proceed with that thorough rinsing procedure that you mastered after the shampooing.

Drying Your Maltese

When your dog has decided he will shake no more, you can help to remove more of that excess water by running your hands gently down your pup's small body and legs like a squeegee. Once confident that you have squeegeed out most of the excess, wrap the wet pup in a towel to soak up even more of the remaining moisture. Be thankful that your Maltese's small size and single coat make this such a relatively quick and easy process.

Now move your wet pet to a warm and comfortable drying area, one with secure footing and away from drafts. Even his crate will do. You can allow your dog to air dry in this warm, draftless space, or you can accelerate the process by blow-drying his coat. With your dog positioned securely on a safe surface, set the hair dryer on warm (not hot), and gently move its airstream back and forth over the coat as you either run your hands or a brush through the hair as it dries. (Note: Do not place the dog in his crate with a stationary *hair dryer* blowing an equally stationary blast of air at the dog, which can result in serious burns and injury.)

If you choose to blow-dry your pup, make sure he is amenable to the noise and the rush of air on his skin and head (again, early introductions can make all the difference). Keep him warm and secure until he is dry, and, once he is, run a quick brush through the coat to prevent mats and tangles. Your grooming session is now almost complete. Besides redoing his topknots, if that is on your agenda, it's time to tend to your pet's teeth, ears, and toenails.

TEETH CLEANING

Teeth cleaning is as important to canine health—especially Maltese canine health—as any other aspect of dog care. Ideally, you should clean your dog's teeth at least twice a week. Use a toothpaste formulated especially for dogs, not people, and a toothbrush designed for dogs as well. Instead, you might wrap a damp cloth around your finger, dip the moistened cloth in the toothpaste, and apply it directly to the dog's teeth. With either technique, use gentle, massaging strokes until all sides of the teeth are clean and bright.

Though it may not be their favorite activity, most dogs can learn to accept this important part of their grooming routine. Teaching them to do so is essential, as is the feeding of dry kibble to keep the teeth clean. Supplement this with professional cleanings by your veterinarian once or twice a year, and you will improve your dog's breath, possibly keep tear staining at bay, and increase your pet's chances of keeping his teeth throughout his lifetime.

TOENAIL CARE

If not trimmed every six to eight weeks, a dog's toenails grow and curve into claw-like appendages that can cause the animal a great deal of discomfort, pain, and lameness. Consequently, the toenails must be trimmed regularly. This is especially critical for the nails of an indoor dog, who walks primarily on soft, carpeted floors that will not naturally wear those toenails down.

Teach your dog to cooperate with nail clipping from an early age (yes, just like every other grooming procedure) by first teaching him to tolerate you touching his toes and playing with his feet. When you are ready to clip the nails, snip only the tip, just where the nail begins to curve. If you cut too deeply, called "quicking," the nail will bleed profusely, so when you take out the nail clippers, take out the styptic pencil or powder, too, just in case. Reward your pet for cooperating, and, if necessary, trim only a few nails per session. Your alternative, of course, is to have the job

done professionally at a veterinary clinic or grooming shop.

CLEANING THE EARS

Inside the flopped, feathered Maltese ears, wax accumulates and fine hair grows. Throw a bit of dirt into the mix, and your busy, active, pampered pet could end up with ear problems: infections, parasites, abrasions—all those lovely troubles. To combat and, preferably, prevent, this, check the inside of his ears regularly, both with your eyes and with your nose. The interior-side surfaces of the ear flaps should appear pink and clean, and they should smell clean, too.

If you spot dirt or wax buildup, or even if you don't, clean the ear gently with a moistened cotton ball or swab, and be sure to wipe up the residual moisture with the dry end of the swab or a dry cloth after cleaning. Moisture can fester within the ear and lead to infection or infestation, so a clean ear must also be a dry ear. Never attempt to clean the delicate interior of the ear canal. Leave that for a competent veterinarian, who should also be contacted whenever you notice your pup shaking his head or scratching incessantly at an ear—the classic signs of ear problems.

MAINTAINING A CLEAN, WHITE FACE

Far too many adorable white Maltese mugs are marred by the stains of a teary eye and a panting tongue. Between baths, pay attention to your Maltese's face to keep staining under control.

In the absence of underlying health conditions that might be to blame for excess tearing and the stains they create, renegade hair falling into those beautiful black eyes may be the root cause of a particular dog's tearing and staining problem. So if your Maltese is looking more like a surly teenager than a cute

puppy, think of what that surly teen's grandmother would advise, and sweep that hair back into topknots or trim the hair back into cute puppy bangs.

A severe case of tearing should be examined by the veterinarian to rule out—or treat—any underlying causes. There may also be a link between dental care and tear staining, so you may be able to help keep tearing and staining at bay by caring diligently for your Maltese's teeth. Medicated eye cleaners are available for use in and around the eyes, but use these only if they are recommended and deemed safe by your pet's doctor.

To maintain a clean, white under-eye area, clean the area regularly. Use a soft brush or small, fine-toothed comb to whisk aside any pesky hairs that may be teasing the eyes, and clean the area to prevent—or clear—any similarly pesky staining that may be taking root there. Moisten a soft clean cloth with warm water and hold it gently over the eye for a few moments like a warm compress (your dog will automatically close his eyes as the cloth approaches). Then remove the cloth, and pat the area dry.

The Maltese's mouth area can also take on a stained appearance, with the dog's food and water supply often being the cause. If, for example, you reside in an area with a high iron content in the water, offer your dog bottled purified or filtered water, and see if that helps. Also, choose a food that is free of artificial colorings that might stain the white hair around your Maltese's mouth. Ideally, this area can also be kept clean and pristine with your pet's routine bathing and grooming schedule.

Training Made Easy

Given the many parallels between successful dog training and child rearing, common-sense child-rearing strategies may actually come in handy when faced with the challenge of teaching a dog to behave properly and reliably within the family pack. Though you cannot expect human learning abilities from your sweet pup, you can employ some of the same techniques that are used to raise children. In the process, you might just find that teaching a Maltese and working toward a common level of understanding can be an unforgettable learning experience.

BASIC TRAINING

Training is an excellent investment in the life of your dog, and your Maltese's training should begin the minute he sets foot in your home. Establish the dog's boundaries quickly through consistent scheduling and repetition, and remember that a dog's entire recipe for contentment is founded on making his owner happy. His instinct, forged from thousands of years spent with the human species, guides his basic desires, telling him that life's greatest rewards are derived from pleasing the "pack leader."

Repetition and reward are critical components in any successful training program, whether you're teaching your dog basic good behavior skills, tricks, or advanced obedience (and yes, Maltese can be obedience champs). Dogs can be taught just about anything you have the patience and ability to teach. This begins with the basics: walking properly on a leash and obeying the sit, stay, come, and down commands, the cornerstones of the well-mannered canine family member.

Training Classes

Proper training begins with owners who remain consistent in, and committed to, teaching commands at home, a situation that can be strengthened by enrolling the dog in formal training classes as well. Such classes are available for dogs of all ages—and all sizes—from puppy kindergarten classes for puppies as young as three or four months to all levels of obedience and specialty classes.

Puppy classes employ training techniques geared toward the developing minds and short attention spans of young dogs. Such a class with a positive, puppy-loving trainer in charge is the ideal place to introduce your puppy—and the puppy's human family—to a lifetime of learning, while at the same time socializing your new family member to a variety of people and other dogs large and small.

An added bonus of any formal training situation is that it permits the student's family members to discuss with the instructor any

special problems or frustrations they may be experiencing with their dog at home. Perhaps the pup is proving to be a bit stubborn in learning the tenets of house-training, maybe a potential barking problem is brewing, or maybe you'd just like some pointers on teaching your Maltese to ask permission before jumping down from the couch so you might help protect his knees. A topflight dog trainer who is getting to know you and your dog should be able to offer personalized advice to help remedy a problem.

From puppy kindergarten, you can move on to more advanced classes that take advantage of a maturing (and mature) dog's expanding skills and attention span, from upper-level obedience classes to agility training, and everything in between. If you decide to work with a professional, find a trainer who uses positive training methods that focus on rewards for positive behavior rather than punishment for failure. Find someone who also has experience working with toy dogs and will view your Maltese as a lively, intelligent little student who wants more from life than simply sitting on a lap.

Consult area experts for referrals: your veterinarian, a local kennel club, your dog's breeder, a well-run animal shelter, and fellow dog owners. Once enrolled, enlist the whole family to participate. Dog training, in truth, is more about training the dog's family than training the dog, since it's the family members who need to learn how to work with the dog both in class and at home. And speaking of home, training only works if you do your homework and practice what you learn in class at home.

BE PREPARED

The operative words for your training regimen should be fun, common sense, and repetition. You are the teacher. You are in control, but if you make it a contest, you'll risk losing and possibly hurting your dog. Tolerance, understanding, repetition, and reward—as well as praise, praise, praise—produce the greatest results. There may at times be a need for a firm scolding, but there is never a need for physical punishment.

Achieving mutual understanding, where you issue clear commands and your dog understands what you are asking of him, is the goal of training—and an important step toward building a strong foundation for your relationship. The ultimate reward comes when your dog responds to your commands and senses that he has pleased you. Sneak learning in when you play, feed, groom, walk, or do anything with your dog, and remember that even the smallest dogs will get bossy if they think they are in control.

When training your dog, voice inflection and volume are very important. Some dogs are intimidated by loud voices but respond well to quiet commands. Find the happy medium and be generous with your praise for proper responses: behaving joyfully, offering a special treat, or scratching your pup behind the ears. On the other hand, turning away or averting your eyes can express disappointment. As a result of your own dramatic performances—and treat rewards (especially for beginning students) as an adjunct to verbal praise and body language—your Maltese can learn when he has pleased you and when he hasn't. Your dog will receive the message of

what you are trying to say, however, only if you offer him immediate praise, so make it easy for him to understand.

First Steps First: Leash Training

One of the first and most important tasks in dog training is teaching your dog to walk on a leash. In leash training you are also teaching your dog to pay attention to you and respond to your commands—an important foundation of all subsequent training.

For this grand endeavor you will need a properly fitting harness and lightweight 6-foot (1.8-m) nylon or leather leash. A harness is the safest option for walking a Maltese, because a leash attached to a traditional buckle neck collar can lead to neck injuries in such a tiny dog. Steer clear, as well, of

extending leashes or chain "choke" collars, the former of which are unnecessary and potentially dangerous and the latter of which almost guarantee injury to the delicate Maltese neck and throat. Your dog should, however, wear his traditional buckle collar with identification tags at all times (loose enough to permit two fingers between collar and neck), even with the harness on a walk, just not with a leash attached.

Once your dog has become accustomed to his harness, snap on the leash and let him drag it around the house to get used to it. This can take a while, even a few days, but once you believe your pup is comfortable with this, pick up your end of the leash and walk around with your little student, applying little or no pressure, permitting your little friend to

lead the way. Gradually increase your control of the leash until you reach the point where you can persuade your puppy to come along in the general direction you choose. The dog has learned that even though the leash restrains and guides, it is nothing to fear, and together you may move on to more advanced levels of the fine art of walking the dog.

Teaching the *Heel* and Beyond

Back in the day, old-school training methods often revolved around the chain choke collar and the "jerk and release" method, where the trainer would deliver commands and "jerk" the chain whenever the dog didn't respond correctly, with the collar then falling loose when he did.

Most trainers today now prefer kinder, gentler methods that not only help the dog gain a better understanding of what is being asked of him but also prevent potential injury to the neck, especially the vulnerable neck of a tiny Maltese. Indeed, though your Maltese may fancy himself a linebacker in a family scrimmage, there remains a delicacy to this breed, and Maltese may at times need to be protected from their own bravado.

You may begin this training off-leash in your home. Hide a treat in your left hand, with your dog positioned on your left side. Walk forward, holding your arm down so your dog, following the treat, naturally walks alongside you at the heel while you say the word "*heel*." Though he may not completely understand what he did, praise him and offer him the treat to let him know he has done something well. Eventually, with that all-important repetition of the process, he will make the connection.

Once you have mastered the task off-leash, it is time to move on to mastering the skill with the leash. Help your dog into his harness, snap on the leash, and position the dog on your left side again. Hold the leash in both hands, with the loop end in your right hand and the midsection in your left, keeping the leash loose and drapey. Walk forward, keeping your dog on your left, and again offer the *heel* command. Your dog may or may not comply (and here, too, a hidden treat or two can help), but in time he should get it.

Teaching the *heel* can take time, but be patient. Keep training sessions short, praise and reward the pup for walking close beside you at the heel, guide him along gently, and resist the urge to yank or pull on the dog. If your dog proves to be a stubborn little student, try walking forward and then quickly turning back in the opposite direction so he has no choice but to turn and follow you (and, when he realizes you intend to do this again and again, he'll have no choice but to watch you very carefully, too). Carry out this technique several times in a row, knowing your dog will not be completely trained in one session, but also knowing you aren't hurting him either.

Walking—or, more appropriately, gaiting—at the heel is a skill the show Maltese must master for the show ring. Pet owners, however, may simply ask that their dogs walk nicely on the leash without pulling (and choking themselves), which, frankly, makes a casual walk with the family more interesting for the family pet. Exercise is as critical to the health, vitality, and emotional stability of a tiny Maltese as it is to his larger cousins. A leisurely, preferably daily, walk—where your pet is permitted to explore, stop and smell the roses, and perhaps even visit with some friendly neighbors and their equally friendly dogs—can, and should, be a highlight of living with a Maltese.

There are as many methods for teaching the basic commands of dog obedience as there are trainers. When the student is a tiny dog like the Maltese, stick to gentle handling, patience, and the knowledge that your dog truly wants to please you. If training at home, the following techniques can be done inside off-leash, or with a loose 6-foot (1.8-m) leash and that trusty harness, which is required if training outdoors in a public place.

Above all, be positive as you teach, and praise and reward your dog—puppy or adult—for understanding what you are asking and responding correctly. Treat rewards can be very effective, starting with treats offered with every command, then tapering off until

the dog doesn't know when he'll be receiving the treat and when he won't. Keep training sessions short; never, ever lose your temper; and remember that you *can* teach an old dog new tricks.

The *Sit*. Sit is a useful and foundational part of your Maltese's course of study and is easy to teach and learn with the student either on- or off-leash. Let's say your little student is named Puffball. Stand facing Puffball as he stands facing you. Show him a treat in your hand, place it over his head near his nose, and slowly move your hand back toward his forehead as you say "Puffball, *sit*." Following the treat back with his eyes and nose, he will have no choice but to sit, after which he will be rewarded profusely with praise and the coveted treat. You can also teach the *sit* by stating the command as you push his rear end down to the floor, but training is usually more effective when the dog believes he is carrying out his mission voluntarily (as though it's his idea), without being forced into position.

The *Down*. A natural offshoot of the sit is the *down* command. With your dog in the *sit* position, again employ the trusty treat. Position the treat again at the dog's nose, move it slowly and vertically down toward the floor as you say "Puffball, *down*." Your little student should again follow the treat down until he finds himself in the *down* position. Praise, praise, praise. (Here, too, you can place your hand on the dog's shoulders and exert gentle pressure down, signaling physically for him to assume the *down* position, but again, the dog who does this on his own may be more effectively trained.)

The *Stay*. A natural offshoot of both the sit and the down is the stay. With the dog in a sitting or down position, place your hand up, palm facing the dog, and say "Puffball, *stay*." Move back a few steps, wait, then return to your student for praise and treating. Begin with brief moments of staying, followed by praise and reward. Then, as he continues to master the command, lengthen both the time he stays and the distance you move back from him as he does so.

The *Come*. Now we face the challenge of teaching your dog to come to you when you call him—a command that, in certain situations, could actually save your pet's life. Once your pup has mastered the *stay* in either the

sit or the *down* position, in a most irresistible style, call your dog to you in a way that convinces him there is nowhere else he would rather be but with you (which, in the case of the Maltese, isn't much of a stretch).

Use treats if you need to, of course, and even if it takes longer than you would like for your dog to obey, always lavish him with praise once he reaches you (never punish, scold, or correct your dog for coming to you when you call him, or he may decide he'd rather not come when called again). As with the *stay*, increase the distance between you and your student as you progress, eventually graduating, perhaps, to a safely enclosed outdoor location with interesting—and distracting—scents and sounds, and always with your dog's safety in mind.

The Case Against Breeding

Once you find yourself under the spell of the enchanting creature
that is the Maltese, you may just realize that you cannot, from that
day forward, live without one. And you may just be right. You may
also believe that you, and the world at large, just can't have too
many Maltese dogs; however, you would be wrong.

TOO MANY DOGS

The sad fact is that the world is filled with far too many dogs who have not been blessed with decent homes—or with homes at all. As adorable and charming as the Maltese is, even this breed has fallen victim to the tragedy of pet overpopulation. It is not at all unusual to find the black button eyes of one of these creatures looking out at prospective adopters from the confines of an animal shelter cubicle or the pages of a Maltese breed rescue website.

As unbelievable as this may sound, these pups are found abandoned on the streets and surrendered every day to shelters and to breed rescue volunteers. People move, children mistreat the tiny family pet, an allergy to dog hair emerges, and the dog finds himself homeless. Many of these so-called secondhand Maltese do ultimately end up in permanent, loving homes, but, sadly, not all of them do.

The message here is that, despite your many friends who may insist that they simply must have a puppy from your beloved Maltese companion (and seem to evaporate into thin air once you have bred said companion and prepared her puppies for promised new homes), breeding is not an endeavor most dog owners should contemplate, let alone pursue. You certainly don't want to add to the numbers of unwanted Maltese out there who may or may not be lucky enough to wind up in worthy homes. But pet overpopulation is only one reason not to breed your Maltese. A dog's health, behavior, longevity, and all-around quality of life are all intimately related to the breeding question. Consider all of these factors before you even imagine making your Maltese pet a parent.

Making the Right Call

The decision to have a Maltese companion surgically altered by spaying or neutering is difficult for some people—too many people, unfortunately—as owners are often too willing to anthropomorphize their pets.

Ideally, the issue is solved by the breeder, who will insist that pet-quality puppies be spayed and neutered and be granted what is known as Limited American Kennel Club registration. The issue will surely be handled by the shelter personnel or rescue group volunteers, with rescuers being adamant about ensuring that their pups be altered before entering their new homes. Nevertheless, there are still those who remain queasy at the thought of spaying and neutering. Here's hoping the following information will help those queasy folks make the right choice.

BENEFITS AND CONSEQUENCES

In making the decision to spay or neuter, one cannot ignore the millions of healthy dogs being destroyed each year for want of responsible owners, or the profound health benefits of altering the family pet. Time and time again, studies have shown—as have dogs themselves—that spayed and neutered pets as a whole live longer, live healthier, and are better companions. These facts alone should override any sense of fear or misguided anthropomorphic nausea that prevents owners from altering their pets.

Spaying

A healthy, intact female comes into heat every six months, and her cycle lasts for about twenty-one days. The resulting mess, the mood swings of the little darling, and the unwanted attentions of neighborhood dogs all typically prove a big nuisance for most pet owners. Of course, this can be easily prevented by having the female spayed, which will have far-reaching benefits.

Spaying is the surgical procedure that prevents canine pregnancy. It can be done at

Papers Aren't Everything

Unfortunately, even in these more enlightened and informed times, when pets are receiving better care than they ever have, far too many people believe that a dog's purebred status—a status verified by those all-important American Kennel Club registration papers—somehow ensures that the dog will always be wanted, loved, and valued. This is not so. Unwanted purebred dogs—even unwanted Maltese—abound in this country. The Humane Society of the United States estimates that at least 25 percent of the dogs in animal shelters are purebreds, and, sadly, Maltese breed rescue organizations coast to coast are kept far too busy in their never-ending efforts to provide a safety net for unwanted Maltese throughout the country.

any time in the female dog's life, beginning at about six months of age (and in some instances, even younger). Not only does spaying prevent the dog from finding herself "with puppy," but it will also reduce her chances of developing mammary cancer, uterine cancer, or life-threatening pregnancy and delivery complications (all too common in tiny dogs). Some also believe that the younger a female dog is spayed—ideally, before her first heat cycle—the better chance she will have of avoiding these maladies later in life.

Neutering

Let's be honest. The male Maltese's role in canine reproduction is not what we might refer to as "life-threatening." Unlike his female counterpart, whose job it is to carry and nurture the puppies, the male does his job early on and is done. But, believe it or not, there are profound health benefits to nipping in the bud the male's ability to play a role in Maltese reproduction.

Neutering, or castration, is a surgical procedure performed on male dogs curtailing their ability to father puppies. In addition, altering a male is recommended to calm a male's aggression and to decrease his wanderlust should he decide to prowl the neighborhood in search of available females (and possibly be hit by a

car in the process). Neutering has also been very effective in reducing a dog's inclination to "mark territory," both inside and outside of the house. The neutered male tends to be a calmer, more attentive companion, enjoying better health and a better quality of life thanks to the potential prevention of testicular cancer and prostatitis.

Dispelling the Myths

Despite the evidence supporting the profound health and lifestyle benefits of spaying and neutering, myths connected to the procedures continue to circulate. The sad result is that far too many dogs are left intact and bred (either intentionally or by accident). Let's take a look at the big three.

71

Myth #1: Spayed and neutered dogs will become fat and lazy. ***Fact:*** While spaying can somewhat slow a female's metabolism, common sense dictates that feeding your pup a fraction less of food and increasing her exercise and playtime can easily counteract any effect spaying might have on that Maltese metabolism.

The same holds true for the neutered male. Neutering will indeed reduce the dog's libido and metabolism, while a smart diet and lots of activity will fill the vacuum. So feed your pup, male or female, responsibly and correctly; avoid excess and unhealthy treats; and make sure your altered pet gets plenty of exercise every day.

Myth #2: A female should be allowed one litter before she is spayed to make her a better pet. ***Fact:*** Aside from the fact that a spayed female is a more even-tempered girl, and thus the "better" pet, pregnancy is a risk for any dog, especially for a tiny dog. Breeding Maltese, then, is best left to those experienced in genetic and bloodline match-making, prenatal care, delivery procedures, and follow-up care.

Backyard breeders who breed their pets also aren't likely to consider the genetic and structural problems that can affect the breed, and, in turn, the puppies they produce. Equally sad are the many puppies placed in mediocre homes by breeders or owners who do not understand the rigorous screening process that the best and most ethical breeders use to ensure their puppies end up with the right people. In short, carrying and delivering puppies does not make a female a better pet any more than fathering puppies makes a male dog a better companion. Spaying and neutering, however, do wield that power.

Myth #3: You can make money breeding your purebred dog. *Fact:* This one always gives the reputable, ethical breeders out there a good laugh. The lives, and checkbooks, of breeders who are devoted to producing the finest examples of their breed are dominated by the costs of prenatal care, genetic tests, registration fees, whelping materials, cleaning and housing supplies, stud fees, ultrasounds, veterinary care…the list goes on. When all is said and done, the costs of breeding the family pet are far greater than the price tag of the puppies—and, in the case of tiny toy dogs, one-puppy litters are quite common.

Final Considerations

The greatest argument in support of protecting your Maltese from parenthood is that breeding toy dogs can be quite dangerous for a tiny dog. Cesarean sections at whelping

time are common with toy dogs, which can result in the loss of puppy, mom, or both. The loss of such a beloved member of the family is simply not worth the risk.

But even if the risks, the cost, and the health benefits can't persuade owners to forgo the breeding of family companions, the most important argument in favor of spaying and neutering is that an altered dog is free to direct more attention toward his or her family rather than toward the cycles and scents of other dogs. The altered dog is more content to remain at home with the people he or she loves, rather than wander the neighborhood in search of potential mates. In other words, altered pets make better pets. And that is a powerful argument indeed!

The Healthy Maltese

Maltese tend to be healthy little dogs, with their robust spirit and vitality shining clearly within their beautiful black eyes. But maintaining this little sprite's health and vitality, and the comfort they foster, doesn't happen automatically. Offer your Maltese the gift of health by educating yourself about canine health and preventive action, by learning what is normal—and abnormal—for your particular pet, and by enlisting the services of a trusted veterinarian.

A VITAL PARTNERSHIP

As the first and best line of defense for your Maltese's health, you need to be ready to act when you suspect all is not well with your little pal. Your mission is to know your dog. Through the maintenance of your pet's daily activities, get to know what is and isn't normal for him physically and emotionally so you might alert the dog's doctor if you suspect trouble is brewing, all in the spirit of early detection and intervention that are the heart of quick and thorough healing.

Your mission also includes finding a veterinarian who is attuned to the needs of a tiny dog and who will handle such a dog with sensitivity and respect. The first logical step to take in the hunt for this coveted practitioner is to get a recommendation from whoever cared for the dog before he came to you—the breeder, shelter volunteer, foster family. Collect names, as well, from the most attentive, nurturing dog owners you know. People who demand only the best care for their dogs will rarely steer you wrong (keep this in mind when you are seeking a doggy day-care facility, a groomer, or a boarding kennel, too), but do your own due diligence as well, since the ultimate decision rests with you and your dog.

CANINE IMMUNIZATIONS

A healthy dog is an immunized dog, but what constitutes the accepted slate of vaccines for dogs has changed somewhat in recent years. Not that long ago, a puppy would begin receiving a series of "puppy shots" at about six weeks of age. These would be followed by repeats of these vaccines

administered every few weeks thereafter, capped at sixteen weeks by the rabies vaccine—the one vaccine typically mandated by local governmental authorities. The dog would then receive annual boosters, with rabies followed up every one to three years, depending on vaccine and community policy.

But as public concerns have mounted over vaccine safety and frequency, the veterinary community has adjusted canine vaccine recommendations. The American Veterinary Medical Association (AVMA) now splits vaccines into two categories: core and non-core vaccines.

The core vaccines include parvovirus, distemper, canine adenovirus, and, of course, rabies. The first three of these, according to the AVMA, should be administered to a puppy

Signs of Illness

Knowing your pet as you do, it is your responsibility to observe and evaluate him daily for even the smallest sign that his health might be at risk. As any veterinarian will tell you, the earlier health conditions are detected, the more easily and effectively they can be treated. Stay alert for the following:

- Loss of appetite
- A change in water consumption (unquenchable thirst can indicate diabetes or kidney problems)
- A change in fecal matter, urine, or frequency of elimination
- Unexplained weight gain or weight loss
- Coughing and choking
- A bloated abdomen (emergency action required)
- An unkempt coat
- Incessant scratching and poor skin condition
- Lumps or bumps
- Head shaking
- Watering eyes
- Limping
- Chronic diarrhea and/or vomiting
- Shivering and restlessness
- Obvious pain
- Blood in feces or urine
- An overall listlessness and change in attitude and behavior

from six to eight weeks of age (ideally eight weeks for a Maltese because of his small size and slow development), followed by repeats every three to four weeks thereafter until the puppy reaches about sixteen weeks of age. Sixteen weeks also marks the age at which the puppy should receive the rabies vaccine (preferably not simultaneously with any other vaccines), followed by the rabies booster annually or every three years after that.

The non-core vaccines are those that target risks inherent in a dog's lifestyle, activities, or region in which the dog lives. The most common of these are the bordatella and parainfluenza vaccines, which are designed to protect dogs from what is known as canine cough (formerly known as kennel cough). This protection is recommended, and usually mandated, for dogs who travel or frequent dog club activities, boarding kennels, and day-care facilities. Also categorized as non-core vaccines are, among others, the vaccines for leptospirosis, coronavirus, and Lyme disease, which many veterinarians now recommend only for dogs who reside where these illnesses are prevalent.

Once the "puppy" vaccines are complete, or once you are assured that a dog with a previously unclear immunization history has been updated (a rescued adult from a shelter, perhaps), work with your veterinarian to design your Maltese's personal vaccination booster schedule. As the caretaker of such a tiny dog, you probably don't wish to barrage his system with more vaccination material than is necessary, so together you can evaluate what and when might be appropriate for your particular pet.

HEREDITARY CONDITIONS

No breed is immune from conditions that might arise from their genetic heritage, and just as the Maltese has inherited an innate understanding of, and affection for, the human species, so has the breed also come into contemporary times with some genetic baggage in tow.

Sound, ethical breeders do all they can to avoid breeding dogs who carry this baggage, but owners are still wise to be aware of the conditions that can emerge in this tiny dog. Such awareness can help you deal with the consequences, should they affect your pet, and help you to prevent those consequences in the first place.

While enthusiasts of virtually every breed can, and do, witness the incidence of conditions such as cleft palate, hypothyroidism, eye problems, and hernias in their dogs, several congenital conditions associated most closely with the Maltese include knee problems, specific respiratory conditions, heart problems, hypoglycemia, and liver shunt disease.

Luxated patellas, or "slipping knee-caps," is a condition in which the dog's kneecaps, as the name implies, dislocates, with the condition usually first making itself known during the dog's first year of life. While most affected Maltese experience a somewhat milder form of the condition, severe and acute cases can require surgery. As with all inherited disorders, the American Maltese Association urges members not to breed affected dogs. In the meantime, owners can reduce the risk of dislocation by, if possible, preventing their Maltese from jumping up on and down from furniture—teaching them

instead, perhaps, to wait for an invitation and their owners' assistance.

Two respiratory conditions seen not all that uncommonly in Maltese are the collapsed trachea and reverse sneezing. ***Collapsed trachea*** is very common in toy dogs, as evident by a cough akin to a "goose honk" that grows more pronounced with age. As discussed earlier in this book, the best way to manage a Maltese whose trachea tends to collapse is to walk the Maltese with a harness rather than a traditional buckle collar, the latter of which can place pressure on the trachea. The affected dog should also see his veterinarian on a regular basis so the doctor

development of the heart muscle, resulting in conditions such as faulty blood oxygenation, coughing, exercise intolerance, fluid buildup in the heart, and heart failure. This is a serious condition, but, depending on severity, some dogs have been known to live with it for years, while others have had it corrected surgically, which can be done with some success by qualified surgeons who specialize in cardiac care.

Hypoglycemia occurs when the body's failure to regulate blood sugars results in a drop in said sugars, causing the dog to stagger, shake, and exhibit signs of listlessness and weakness as well as pale gums. The condition is rather common in toy breeds, an episode of which can be triggered by picky or irregular eating habits, overexcitement, vaccinations, liver shunt disease (see below), extreme temperatures, stress, illness, and parasites. Manage it by learning how, with veterinary instruction, to correct the sugar levels should an episode occur and—as the American Maltese Association recommends—by keeping puppies with mom until they reach twelve weeks of age and develop a solid nutritional foundation.

Maltese can also be affected by a condition known as *liver shunt disease*, in which blood vessels fail to carry the dog's blood through the liver to be cleansed of toxins. Needless to say, an affected Maltese is a sick little puppy, very small and typically exhibiting a variety of physical and behavioral signs, including digestive problems, aggression, and seizures. Some cases have been treated with drug therapies to varying degrees of success, but a preferable remedy would be to prevent

can keep tabs on the severity and progression of the condition.

You can recognize *reverse sneezing* in a dog who seems to be choking and/or gasping for air. Caused by a spasm in the dog's throat, this then leads to rapid breathing, snorting, and wheezing sounds. Within a minute or two, the spasm should subside, and the dog will be breathing normally again. Though dramatic and unpleasant to witness, reverse sneezing is not inherently dangerous, and its incidence might be reduced by preventing the dog from pulling on the leash (again, remember that trusty harness), eating and drinking too quickly, or becoming overly excited.

The most common *heart problems* in Maltese include heart murmurs and a condition known as *patent ductus arteriosus*. The latter condition, PDA, involves an improper

Why a Twelve-Week Waiting Period?

The American Maltese Association endorses (and formalizes within its Code of Ethics) the recommendation that puppies not leave their mothers and siblings to begin life with their new human families until twelve weeks of age—four weeks later than the eight weeks typically accepted as the norm within the dog world.

The Maltese, you see, is somewhat of a late bloomer (and a late weaner)—with his teeth coming in and, thus, his normal eating abilities and habits kicking in a few weeks later than we see in many other breeds. Twelve weeks also permits the dog's tiny bladder—and thus his control of that bladder—to mature a bit, so that house-training in his new home may go more smoothly than it would at eight weeks of age.

Those few extra weeks afford this tiny dog a little extra growth time, making his transition to a new and unfamiliar environment just that much safer and that much more relaxed, and because the pup has ample time to start eating solid food, he may be less prone to hypoglycemia. Such timing also helps to ensure that the youngster can be safely vaccinated at least once—possibly twice—before joining his new family. In short, good things come to those who wait!

it altogether by avoiding the breeding of affected dogs.

EXTERNAL PARASITE CONTROL

Once upon a time, information on external parasites—in particular, flea control—would appear most logically in a book like this in the chapter on grooming. But the veritable revolution that has taken place in canine flea control since those bygone times makes this topic more appropriately included in a chapter on health and medicine.

During that once-upon-a-time era, owners had only a rather pedestrian, even primitive, option for the control of these little blood-suckers, which always seemed to leave the flea with the upper hand, free to cause itching and flea-bite allergies to its heart's content. A three-pronged attack was in order (and still is), but it was all done externally in a never-ending chase, following fleas around to prevent them from accessing a particular dog, home, and yard. The revolution occurred when researchers came up with pharmaceutical options, some that attack fleas in their pre-adult stages before they ever even have a chance to enjoy a blood meal from a canine host, and some—applied to the skin—that poison adult fleas that dare to take a bite from an unsuspecting, though treated, dog.

These products are most safely available by prescription, and indeed you will want your veterinarian's input and approval, as the choice of product depends on each particular dog's age, size, lifestyle, and special needs and sensitivities. Some of these products are ingested and some are applied topically to the

grooming routine of weekly baths and daily brushing and combing to keep your Maltese pristine and flea-free.

Unfortunately, fleas are not the only wee vampires that may target your darling dog. Ticks and mites can also wreak havoc, the former potentially transmitting such serious illness as Lyme disease and Rocky Mountain spotted fever, the latter of which causes chronic skin problems, scratching, and head shaking. The good news is that some of the concoctions designed to fight fleas can also help control ticks and mites as well—which is especially helpful if you reside or travel in areas where, say, Lyme disease is prevalent, or you have a rescued Maltese that came to you from a shelter situation where mite infestations have been identified.

Tread cautiously, however, with the products you choose and the regimen you follow in your war waged against external parasites. The Maltese, as we have seen, is a very small dog who can be highly sensitive to chemicals and environmental allergens. Use these powerful products only as directed and only as needed, and watch carefully for any adverse reactions—breathing difficulties, itchy skin, digestive troubles—they might cause in your dog.

INTERNAL PARASITE PREVENTION

As unpleasant as it is to ponder, dogs are also appealing hosts for parasites of the internal kind. A variety of these, primarily worms, can gain access even to a dog receiving top-notch care, so keep an eye open for the signs, and be ready to treat if necessary.

skin between the dog's shoulder blades. Some are offered monthly, some more frequently.

If you suspect fleas have gained a foothold on your Maltese—and you see them scampering around on your dog's belly or simply spot the tell-tale specks of flea dirt (flea excrement) on your pup's skin—you can assume that fleas are in your home and yard as well. While tending to your dog's infestation with a flea bath and proper follow-up treatment to prevent future fleas, treat your home and yard as well with products designed for environmental use. Supplement this with a sound

The most obvious signs of infestation of an internal parasite are found in the dog's feces, sometimes to the naked eye (as in tapeworms, which are transmitted by fleas and appear as rice-like segments in a dog's stool), or detected microscopically by a veterinarian in stool samples that indicate the presence of **roundworms**, **hookworms**, and **whipworms**.

Your veterinarian should ask for a stool sample from your dog once or twice a year to make sure all is clear internally. In the meantime, watch for the classic signs of potential infestation—loss of appetite, blood in the stools, listlessness, poor coat quality, etc.—and take it seriously, as a severe infestation can take a toll on dogs of all ages. Once detected, however, intestinal worms can usually be eradicated easily, especially if discovered and treated early.

One type of worm not so easily conquered is the **heartworm**, which is transmitted by mosquito and takes up residence in its host's heart. Oral heartworm preventives are usually administered monthly, but only after a blood test indicates that the dog is heartworm-free. Some preventives are formulated to prevent heartworms in addition to intestinal parasites and even fleas, but, again, preventives are best chosen with veterinary input for the safety of your particular dog. Treatment for a heartworm infestation is quite brutal for the patient, so prevention is certainly preferable and more humane.

Single-Celled Parasites

Single-celled protozoa are another type of parasite that can find their way into a dog's system and wreak havoc with the digestive tract. **Coccidia** takes advantage of filthy, overcrowded living conditions (as one might find in high-density, warehouse-style puppy mills), and **giardia** can exist in lakes and reservoirs from which dog and owner might take a drink while hiking and camping (and, yes, Maltese have been known to hike and camp). Treatment of coccidia requires specialized antibiotic therapy coupled with a move to a more sanitary environment, while giardia, once diagnosed, requires specialized medications and plenty of fluids, a treatment plan that the dog's owner will probably require as well.

KEEPING FIT

We really can't make our way through a chapter on Maltese health without touching on the subject of exercise. Yes, the Maltese is a toy dog, but he is still a dog, and all dogs

need exercise if they are to reap the benefits of long-term health and well-being.

You might think that people choose a Maltese as a pet simply so they can install the pampered pet on a satin pillow, ply him with bon-bons and ice cream, and sit back to bask in his beauty. Do that, and your little white friend won't be around for long.

Maltese are fun-loving, adventurous little creatures. They want and need activity in the company of the people they love. Many a Maltese enjoys such canine activities as obedience training and agility, but your exercise program need not be so formal. Keep it simple, keep it fun, and make it part of the daily routine, starting with daily walks. You'd be hard pressed to find a Maltese who doesn't love a daily walk with his owner or, better yet, his entire family—evident as he jumps for joy as soon as you just glance at the leash hanging by the front door.

Despite such love of activity, however, the Maltese is a bonafide inside dog—and a tiny one at that. When he does venture outside, make sure he is on a leash and supervised at all times. Protect your little guy from the dangers that might lurk in the great outdoors, such as children who have not been schooled in canine protocols, other dogs, coyotes, oncoming cars and bicycles, and, yes, even birds of prey.

Those familiar with the hilarious film "The Proposal" might remember the scene where a white puppy is lifted into the air within the clutches of an eagle. Though the scene is played for laughs, and though the small white puppy (not a Maltese) is safely returned to earth, there is truth in the message it conveys, so don't let that movie scene become a reality.

THE TIME TO SAY GOOD-BYE

The only true downside of having a dog in your life is the sad fact that dogs don't live as long as we do. It may be five years, or it may be fifteen, but the day will come all too soon when you have to say good-bye.

One of the most difficult responsibilities of dog ownership is making the decision to end the life of an old friend who is suffering, and, sadly, most of us who have lived with dogs have had to do this at one time or another.

When faced with this decision, ask yourself the following questions: Is life still rewarding and comfortable for your pet? Can he still get up and down without pain, move without discomfort, eat sufficiently, and eliminate without a problem? Sometimes all a dog has left is his dignity, and he trusts the people he loves to ensure that his dignity remains intact. If your dog can no longer exist within the dignified boundaries he has enjoyed all his life as a member of your family, then life probably has become sadly unpleasant for him. You must then do what is decent and, with the help of your veterinarian, end his suffering as humanely as possible.

When you make this courageous decision, spend some time remembering the happy times you have spent with your beautiful little friend and all the memorable moments you have shared. Try not to dwell on the loss, but instead celebrate the relationship and all that this sweet spirit has brought to your life. Dig out old photographs and recall the funny antics, the cute habits, and the brilliant tricks that made your Maltese so very special.

Once your pet is gone, give yourself time to heal and to grieve, but don't deny yourself

happiness because of the possibility of future pain. We've all heard people claim, in the wake of a beloved pet's death, that there will be no more dogs in the household. It's just too painful when it's time for them to go. But when you do decide to take the plunge again (and people who have lived happily with dogs usually can't remain dogless forever), remember that no dog can ever take the place of the dog you have just lost, and it's not fair to expect that of a new dog who enters your household. Yet a new ball of fluff can, and will, find a vacant little spot in your heart, right next to the spot occupied by the dog who came, and was loved, before.

Though small in stature, the adventurous little sprite that is the Maltese is no stranger to circumstances that might find him in need of first-aid. What follows is a brief introduction to some of the more common conditions that may require you to act quickly before you can get your dog to the veterinarian.

Bleeding wounds. While bleeding is the body's natural way of cleansing a wound, there is a big difference between a small, superficial cut and a bleeding wound. The latter requires your immediate attention, as you may need to get the bleeding under control before taking the dog to the veterinarian.

First, cover the wound with a clean cloth, towel, or gauze. Apply direct pressure with your fingers, which may be all that is required to stop the flow. Remove the material every thirty seconds to check if the flow has stopped. If it doesn't stop, or if it spurts (the sign of an arterial wound), wrap more layers of material firmly around the wound and get the dog to the veterinarian immediately.

Shock. Shock is the body's response to such serious health conditions as broken bones or massive blood loss. Here, too, you must get your pet's condition under control so you can get him to the animal hospital for treatment.

If, following a trauma, the dog is lying quietly with a weak but rapid pulse, shallow breathing, a low body temperature, and pale gums, death could be imminent if you don't act quickly. Keep the dog calm and comfortable, and place a blanket over him to keep him warm. Get any bleeding under control, and then transport the dog to the veterinarian as soon as possible without jarring him too dramatically, especially if you suspect broken bones or internal injuries (a task much easier to handle with a Maltese, of course, than with a larger dog). In most cases of shock, only a veterinarian is qualified to administer the treatment necessary to reverse the potentially life-threatening condition.

Choking. Maltese are curious little critters, and it is not unusual for one to find an interesting item on the floor and grab it with his teeth, only to have it lodge in his throat and block his airway. If you notice your dog opening his mouth as if to vomit, salivating, and/or pawing at his mouth with his paws, he may be choking.

If the dog is still breathing, get him to the veterinarian immediately. If, however, he stops breathing and loses consciousness, pry his jaws open with the back of a screwdriver or similar item, and try to see the offending object. You may be able to remove the object with needle-nose pliers or tweezers. There is also a canine version of the Heimlich maneuver, but you will need to go over this with your veterinarian to ensure you know how to do it safely with such a small dog—before you ever need to use it.

Poisoning. Curiosity has killed as many dogs as cats, so keep the number of your local poison control center posted prominently in your home should the day come when you need it—and need it quickly. There are as many remedies for poisoning as there are types of poison. If you suspect poisoning, try to identify what your dog may have ingested or contacted so you can inform the veterinarian or poison control official of that vital information in the event of an emergency. Wiser still is the owner who takes action to prevent poisoning, such as keeping pesticides and other poisons away from a curious Maltese and making sure the family pet never has access to such sweet-smelling, sweet-tasting poisons as antifreeze.

Heatstroke. Maltese owners find it very difficult to leave their precious pets behind—even if that means leaving the dog in a car on a warm day. Even if the weather doesn't seem extraordinarily hot, the dog can still experience heatstroke, a condition that can turn fatal very quickly.

If you notice your Maltese panting excessively and perhaps panicking and having trouble standing, you need to get him cooled down gradually. Remove the dog from direct sunlight (preferably into an air-conditioned room), and immerse your pet in a tub of cool (not cold) water. Encourage him to drink small rations of cool water—out of your hand if necessary—and, as with any emergency, get the patient to the animal hospital as soon as possible, even if he seems to have recovered.

Heatstroke is, of course, another emergency that can be prevented. Leave your Maltese at home on warmer days, and remember that a mild temperature in a car can heat up to scalding in minutes. Even an open window or two may not sufficiently cool the car, and it leaves your dog at risk of being stolen. Take your walks and jogs with your pet during the cooler times of the day, and make sure that all day, every day, he has access to fresh, cool water and an escape from direct heat and sunlight.

Fun and Games

Whether you're talking a 5-pound (2.3 kg) Maltese or a 110-pound (50 kg) Malamute, dogs are dogs, and they just want to have fun. You can satisfy the longings of your tiny pup's quest for activity through either formal activities or informal fun that you design yourself, resulting in a tighter bond between dog and owner and a healthier dog.

FOR EVERY DOG: WALKING AND PLAYING

What every dog needs—and what almost every dog loves—are daily walks with the people they call family. Their legs may be short, their volume almost nil, but toy dogs also deserve to go out and about to explore the world, sniff the grass, and inhale the fresh air. Such activity not only stimulates their mind and body, but it also keeps them young and spry, and, if pursued properly, socialized.

Train your dog at an early age to walk on a leash. Outfit your little friend with a 4- to 6-foot (1.2–1.8 m) leash, and instead of connecting that leash to his traditional buckle collar, which he should wear at all times for identification purposes, teach him to wear a harness for his walks. Harnesses, which are available in a variety of styles and colors, can provide toy dogs with a sense of security, while at the same time protecting their small necks from any tugging that might occur when a leash is connected to a neck collar.

To make walking the dog as safe and pleasant as possible, make sure your dog remains on his leash at all times; allow your little dog to visit only with people, pets and kids who you know are unquestionably trustworthy; and watch for potential dangers (snarling dogs, careening skateboarders, etc.) so you can cross the street or pick up your tiny pet before worlds collide. Because Maltese are known for grass allergies, when you return from your walk, clean your pup's feet with either a damp cloth or quick soak (and dry them gently and thoroughly afterwards). This can help remove any pollens or other allergens the dog may have brought home with him.

Game playing, from fetch to hide-and-seek, can be pretty irresistible to most Maltese, as can playing with other dogs if all the playmates, including the Maltese, are properly socialized. You might consider taking your Maltese to the local dog park, but proceed with caution. Your wee pup may indeed possess the heart of a lion, but his size remains that of a squirrel. He may, without a hint of hesitation, step boldly into the heart of the dog park with a pack of dogs who outweigh him by 90 pounds, but you, in turn, may have to intervene for his own protection. Even if all those large dogs accept him with affection, he could end up trampled and inadvertently injured.

Your tiny dog might more safely play with others of his kind at a clean, well-run doggy day-care facility that offers small dogs their own room or enclosure. Take stock of friends and family who own small dogs as well, and perhaps, if all are healthy and properly socialized, assemble your own small- and tiny-dog playgroup that meets at a clean and secure location on a weekly basis. And just as you would bring cookies for a toddler playgroup, the dog moms and dads for your puppy playgroup can all take turns bringing the dog biscuits.

THE CONFIRMATION SHOW RING

With that long, flowing coat and sparkling black eyes, the Maltese is indeed a quintessential show dog. If showing in the confirmation show ring is of interest to you, attend as many shows as you can and find a mentor (ideally a breeder who, impressed by your interest, works with you to shepherd one of his or her show prospects into the ring).

Successful show dogs are carefully bred to meet the highest standards of structure, temperament, and health; religiously trained to conduct themselves properly in the show ring; meticulously groomed for snow-white splendor; and skillfully presented in the ring to the judges. Judges inspect and evaluate all parts of the dog, from nose to tail, so in addition to being trained to gait properly beside his handler, the little champion must also learn to tolerate the judge's hands-on attention.

To compete in the confirmation show ring, a dog must be an intact purebred and be show-ring trained to show off his innate charm and sparkle. Confirmation showing is a serious, often expensive, commitment, but as with all canine activities, it can lead to lifelong friendships, while providing all involved with an unmatched avenue for celebrating the dogs they love.

OBEDIENCE, AGILITY, CITIZENSHIP, AND THERAPY

While confirmation showing is for those dogs who most closely meet their breed standard, virtually any purebred, even the tiniest purebred, can be trained to compete in *obedience trials*, where attention is focused on dog-and-handler teamwork and performance. As smart and enthusiastic as they are, Maltese can do incredibly well in obedience trials, and they are very popular with spectators, who don't expect such adorable little puffballs to perform so expertly. Do not, then, underestimate your Maltese's ability to acquire the title of Obedience Champion.

Agility is a popular sport in which dogs, in partnership with their owners, traverse a challenging obstacle course in an activity that promotes fun, exercise, and bonding. Coached by their human partners, agility athletes leap, crawl, and climb to their hearts' delight, with the events proving to be as exciting for the spectators as they are for the participants.

The American Kennel Club has also developed a program to encourage all owners to train their dogs properly. This program, the *Canine Good Citizen Test* (CGCT) emphasizes responsible dog ownership and proper canine behavior by testing a dog's ability to demonstrate his ability to pass such tests as greeting a friendly stranger, obeying basic commands, and sitting quietly for grooming. Dogs of any age, purebred or mixed breed, can take the multi-step CGCT, earn a certificate of accomplishment from the AKC, and have the title Canine Good Citizen added to their names.

And speaking of good canine citizenship, you might also consider training your Maltese to become a *registered therapy dog*. Therapy dogs visit elderly people in nursing homes, troubled children in schools, and patients of all ages confined to hospitals, with the animals' mere presence promoting human health and healing. Therapy dogs must be beautifully behaved, healthy, obedient, and affectionate toward humans. Therapy dog organizations exist in most areas and arrange the visits as well as help to prepare and train owners and their dogs for patient visits.

Whether your Maltese has an obedience career in his future, a calling for community service, or simply a life dedicated to pleasing his family makes no difference to the dog. The true measure of the quality of the human-dog relationship lies in mutual contentment and respect.

Dogs are the most versatile of companions, and we have been most fortunate to have shared a rich and affectionate relationship with them that dates back tens of thousands of years. Beyond any formal dog activities you might share with your pet, your Maltese is your faithful friend when you are in need of companionship, lending a feathered, flopped ear to listen to all you have to say and always finding you brilliant and wonderful. The Maltese's most precious title, then, is that of family champion, earned as he scampers across the living room floor to greet you joyfully at the end of each day.

Information

PUREBRED DOG RESOURCES

American Maltese Association
www.americanmaltese.org

The American Kennel Club
www.akc.org
8051 Arco Corporate Drive, Suite 100
Raleigh, NC 27617-3390
(919) 233-9767

PetMaltese.com
(Maltese Information Center)
www.petmaltese.com

MALTESE BREED RESCUE

American Maltese Association Rescue
www.americanmalteserescue.org

Maltese Rescue California
www.malteserescuecalifornia.org

Metropolitan Maltese Rescue
www.malteserescue.com
P.O. Box 20395
New York, NY 10011

Southern Comfort Maltese Rescue
www.scmradoption.com
P.O. Box 2005
Chattanooga, TN 37409

CANINE ACTIVITY ORGANIZATIONS

AKC Canine Good Citizen Program
*http://www.akc.org/dogowner/training/
    canine_good_citizen/*

The North American Dog Agility Council
www.nadac.com
66955 Gist Road
Bend, OR 97701

Teacup Dogs Agility Association
(Agility events for "dogs of small stature")
www.k9tdaa.com
P.O. Box 48
Waterford, OH 45786

Therapy Dogs International
www.tdi-dog.org
88 Bartley Road
Flanders, NJ 07836

United States Dog Agility Association
www.usdaa.com
P.O. Box 850955
Richardson, TX 75085

BOOKS

American Kennel Club. The New Complete
    Dog Book: Official Breed Standards and
    All New Profiles for 200 Breeds, 21st ed.
    California: i-5 Publishing, 2014.
Arden, Darlene. Small Dogs, Big Hearts:
    A Guide to Caring for Your Little Dog
    (Revised Edition). New York: Howell Book
    House, 2006.
Linden, Bobbie. The Maltese: An Owner's
    Guide to a Happy, Healthy Pet. New York:
    Howell Book House, 1998.
Wood, Deborah. The Little Dogs' Activity
    Book: Fun and Frolic for a Fit Four-Legged
    Friend. New Jersey: TFH Publications,
    2007.

Index

and his fondness for the little ones is reflected in this tribute to the Maltese.

Betsy Siino is an award-winning author who has written hundreds of articles and more than two dozen books on animals and their care. Having herself been raised by Maltese, some of her fondest memories include sneaking these adorable dogs into restaurants, airports, hotels, shopping malls, and wherever else dogs are allegedly not allowed. Betsy lives and writes on the West Coast with her family, including her current white fluffy companion, Kody the Samoyed.

Acknowledgments

The Maltese breed has always been very dear to me, and I am grateful for this opportunity to share information on this dynamic little dog. In this spirit, many thanks to all who contributed to the first edition of this book, and to Beth Savage of Metropolitan Maltese Rescue, and to the late Mary Dube', co-founder of Southern Comfort Maltese Rescue, who helped to ensure the second edition would also be a valuable addition to the Maltese world. On a personal level, I thank as always my family—Michael, Chris, Jenny and Kody—and, of course, Tiger, my first oh-so-legendary Maltese, who started it all.

—Betsy

About the Authors

Joe Fulda was, for many years, one of America's most respected canine authorities. A distinguished member of the Dog Writers Association of America, he was happiest when he could help others learn more about dogs or how to better care for their dogs. Joe Fulda had a special affection for the toy breeds

Important Note

This pet owner's manual tells the reader how to buy or adopt, and care for, a Maltese. The author and publisher consider it important to point out that the advice given in the book is meant primarily for normally developed dogs of excellent physical health and sound temperament.

Anyone who acquires a fully-grown dog should be aware that the animal has already formed its basic impressions of human beings. The new owner should watch the animal carefully, including its behavior toward humans, and, whenever possible, should meet the previous owner.

Caution is further advised in the association of children with dogs, in meeting with other dogs, and in exercising the dog without a leash.

Even well-behaved and carefully supervised dogs sometimes do damage to someone else's property or cause accidents. It is therefore in the owner's interest to be adequately insured against such eventualities, and we strongly urge all dog owners to purchase a liability policy that covers their dog.

Cover Photos

Photo Credits

A Note on Pronouns

Many dog lovers feel that the pronoun "it" is not
appropriate when referring to a beloved pet. For this
reason, Maltese are referred to as "he" throughout this
book, unless the topic specifically relates to female
dogs. No gender bias is intended by this writing style.

All inquiries should be addressed to:
Barron's Educational Series, Inc.
250 Wireless Boulevard
Hauppauge, NY 11788
www.barronseduc.com

ISBN: 978-1-4380-0481-5

**Library of Congress Cataloging-in-Publication
Data**
Fulda, Joe.
 Maltese : everything about purchase, care, nutrition,
behavior, and training / Joe Fulda and Betsy Siino. —
3rd edition.
     pages cm — (A complete pet owner's manual)
 "Everything about purchase, care, nutrition,
behavior, and training."
 Includes bibliographical references and index.
 ISBN 978-1-4380-0481-5 (alk. paper)
 1. Maltese dog. I. Siino, Betsy. II. Title.
SF429.M25F85 2015
636.76—dc23
                                    2014045286

Printed in China
9 8 7 6 5 4 3 2 1